NEW ELEMENTS:
the story of
MARIE CURIE

NEW ELEMENTS:
the story of
MARIE CURIE

Della Yannuzzi

MORGAN REYNOLDS

PUBLISHING

Greensboro, North Carolina

Profiles
IN SCIENCE

Robert Boyle
Rosalind Franklin
Ibn al-Haytham
Edmond Halley
Marie Curie
Antonio Meucci
Caroline Herschel

NEW ELEMENTS: THE STORY OF MARIE CURIE

Copyright © 2006 by Della Yannuzzi

Library of Congress Cataloging-in-Publication Data

Yannuzzi, Della A.
  New elements : the story of Marie Curie / by Della Yannuzzi. -- 1st ed.
    p. cm.
  Includes bibliographical references and index.
  ISBN-13: 978-1-59935-023-3 (lib. bdg.)
  ISBN-10: 1-59935-023-8 (lib. bdg.)
  1. Curie, Marie, 1867-1934. 2. Women chemists--Poland--Biography. 3.
Chemists--Poland--Biography. I. Title.
  QD22.C8Y364 2006
  540.92--dc22
  [B]

                                              2006018887

Printed in the United States of America
First Edition

In memory of my mother, Mary,
and grandmother, Anna

Contents

Marie Curie.
(Courtesy of the Granger Collection.)

one

A GIRL CALLED MANYA

Marie Curie learned how to concentrate at an early age. Growing up in a bustling household in Warsaw, Poland, in the 1870s, she had to learn how to focus her attention and ignore distractions. Manya, as she was called, was a shy, intelligent girl with a good memory. Once her older sister Bronya was trying to read a lesson but was having trouble with the words. Four-year-old Manya impatiently snatched the book away and began to read aloud. Her parents and siblings were surprised; they did not know she could read. Manya, afraid she had done something wrong, cried out, "Beg pardon! I didn't do it on purpose."

Manya's siblings were intelligent too, but they had to work a little harder at their studies. They thought Manya's concentration skills were unusual and liked to play jokes on her. After dinner one evening, Manya and her siblings sat around the large dining table doing their homework, reading, and talking. Manya sat in her favorite position with both elbows resting on the table and her hands beneath her chin, a book open on the table in front of her. When the voices around the table grew too loud, Manya clapped her hands over her ears. Two of her sisters, Bronya and Hela, and a cousin, Henrietta Michalowska, crept up behind Manya and began to build a tower of chairs around her. They placed two chairs on either side, one behind, two on top of those, and one more on top to form a pyramid. Then the girls tiptoed away and waited for Manya to notice the ring of chairs. When Manya at last closed her book and stood up, she hit her head against the top chair, sending the entire arrangement crashing around her. The sisters laughed, but Manya just walked past them, muttering: "That's stupid!"

Strong-willed Manya would be well served in the future by that special ability to concentrate, when she became the Nobel Prize-winning scientist Marie Curie.

Manya's full name was Marya Salomee Sklodowska. When she was born on November 7, 1867, in Russian-controlled Poland, she was the fifth and youngest child born into a family of three girls and a boy. All of her siblings had nicknames. Her eldest sister Sophie, born in 1860, was called Zosia. The only boy, born in 1863, was named Joseph but called Jozio. Bronislawa, named after her mother, was born in 1865 and called Bronya. Helena, born in 1866, was known as Hela.

Manya's parents, Bronislawa and Wladyslaw Sklodowski, also came from large families. Manya's mother worked

The Sklodowski siblings: Zosia, Hela, Manya, Jozio, and Bronya. (Courtesy of the Association Curie et Joliot-Curie, Paris.)

as the director of a private girls' school, and her father was a mathematics and physics teacher who spoke several languages. Education and preparing for a career were important goals in the Sklodowski family. Unfortunately, there were fewer opportunities for girls than for boys. Manya's brother Jozio would get to attend the University of Warsaw, but girls were denied higher education in Poland. Their formal education ended at age fifteen or sixteen.

When Manya was a child, Poland was divided between Russia, Austria, and Prussia. Warsaw and the land to the east was controlled by Russia and over the decades there had been several uprisings against the hated Russian troops. Four years before Manya was born, in January of 1863, thousands of Polish nationalists were killed or captured after taking up arms against Russia. Manya's uncle was wounded in the uprising and spent four years in a Siberian prison.

POLAND AND RUSSIA

Poland was once one of the largest and most powerful countries in Europe. It had an early constitution written to protect the social classes from monarchial power. But in the eighteenth century Poland's political structure weakened, and it became a target for its more powerful neighbors, Russia, Prussia, and Austria. In 1772, these three kingdoms seized 81,000 square miles of Poland, which were never retuned to Polish control.

In the early 1800s, Napoleon Bonaparte tried to help with the formation of a small Polish state, but when Napoleon was defeated by Russia, Poland reverted back into the hands of its occupiers. Czar Alexander I imposed draconian laws upon the Polish people that required them to learn the Russian language, customs, and rules. If they were caught speaking Polish they were punished or fined. Most Polish children attended Russian-controlled schools; some did not even attend school because their parents did not want them to learn this foreign language.

In 1830, and again in 1863, the Poles rose up in rebellion. Both times they were crushed by Russian forces. Families lost lands they had owned for hundreds of years. Marie Curie's grandfather fought in the 1830 uprising and had been captured by the Russians. He was later released to resume his life in Warsaw but the family land was never regained.

When Marie was born, Alexander II was the czar of Russia. He remained in this position until he was assassinated in 1881. Marie was fourteen when the czar's son, Alexander III, became the new ruler. Alexander III was a ruthless ruler who further suppressed political and social expression. The last czar of Russia was Nicholas II, Alexander III's son, who was both unpopular and weak. In 1918 he and his wife Alexandra and their five children were killed by the Bolshevik Communists who seized power in Russia in 1917.

Poland regained its independence from Russia in 1918, at the end of World War I. In 1921, Poland and the Soviet Union signed a peace treaty, but the distrust still ran deep. Then, in 1939, Nazi Germany invaded Poland to set off World War II. The Soviet Union, which was composed of Russia and other republics under Communist control and had previously signed an agreement with Germany, also invaded in 1939.

After the war and the defeat of Nazi Germany, a Soviet-dominated Communist government controlled Poland for decades. Then, in the 1980s, a national resistance movement led by a confederation of trade unions called Solidarity was formed, and the Communist government collapsed in 1990. Soon after, Poland held democratic elections.

By law, Poles had to speak Russian in public. From an early age Manya learned to speak the hated language of the occupiers and to always be mindful of her actions. Russian spies, working for the government, lurked everywhere. No one was permitted to criticize the government. Russian inspectors paid regular visits to the schools, where they drilled students on their knowledge of Russian language and history. Manya was often called upon to answer the inspectors' questions because she spoke the Russian language well and was able to memorize history lessons. Manya disliked these drills, but she had a duty to help her teacher and classmates pass the inspections. Manya and her family, like many other Polish families living under Russian rule, pretended allegiance to the foreign government. In the privacy of their homes, they remained loyal Polish citizens.

Manya's father, in particular, suffered the effects of Russian dominance in order to support his family. He secured a good position at a boys' high school teaching physics and mathematics. The family moved from a small apartment on Freta Street to a new apartment on Nowolipki Street, farther from the center of Warsaw. Manya's mother, whose health was poor, decided that her commute to work was now too long and that her children needed her at home and resigned her position at the girls' school. In order to save on expenses, she taught herself to make shoes for her children.

Outwardly, Manya's father pretended to follow Russian rules by working within the confines of the government. But he could not entirely hide his Polish patriotism and often clashed with school directors and inspectors over the suppression of Polish customs, history, and language. He eventually lost his job because his Russian supervisor suspected him of promoting Polish nationalism. When Manya was older, she often said that her father could have had a brilliant teaching career if his ideas had been accepted by the government.

Freta Street in Warsaw, Poland. Manya was born in the building to the left with a balcony. (Maria Sklodowska-Curie Museum, Warsaw)

Manya's home life changed after her father lost his job. He had previously made some bad investments with a family member and lost most of his savings. He decided to teach student boarders rather than work in another government school. Because Professor Sklodowski was an excellent teacher, there was no shortage of boarders and Manya's home was soon filled with noisy boys reciting their lessons, roughhousing, and playing tricks on her because of her studious nature. Manya liked quiet and privacy, but there was little of either in the Sklodowski household. Because the boys took up so much space, Manya could not have a room of her own and slept on a couch in the dining room.

Bronislawa Sklodowska, Manya's mother, as the Freta Street School headmistress.
(Courtesy of the Association Curie et Joliot-Curie, Paris.)

The mostly Polish boarders brought in much-needed money, but they also brought in illness. When Manya was about five years old, her mother contracted tuberculosis, a bacterial infection of the lungs. At the time, there was no medicine to treat the disease. Doctors thought rest and fresh air were the best remedies. Bronislawa did not want her children to contract the incurable disease and did not hug or kiss them or allow them to sit on her lap. Manya's eldest sister Zosia became their mother's caretaker. They were often away from home, traveling to Nice, France and other places where Bronislawa could bathe in salt water and breathe the fresh air off the ocean.

Despite her precautions, illness still struck at home. Manya's sisters, Bronya and Zosia, caught typhus from one of the boarders and fell gravely ill from the bacterial infection. Bronya recovered, but Zosia died at age fourteen. Manya's mother suffered greatly at the loss of her eldest child, and two years later she herself died from the tuberculosis. Manya was only ten years old.

Although the family grieved for the loss of their mother and sister, they remained close. Before her mother's death, Manya and her sister Hela had been enrolled in a private girls' school headed by a caring woman named Jadwiga Sikorska. Madame Sikorska followed the Russian rules, but in private she allowed her students to speak the Polish language and encouraged the study of Polish culture, history, and geography. Manya continued her studies at this school until the director told her father that he should wait a year before enrolling Manya in the fourth grade. The director explained that while Manya was capable of doing the work, she seemed to be suffering emotionally from the deaths of her sister and mother. Instead of following this advice, Manya's father took her from the school and placed her in a government school. His reasons for doing so were never explained.

Manya did well in the government school, even though it

was a stressful environment. The Russian inspectors drilled the Polish girls frequently and everyone was required to speak Russian. Manya was called upon frequently because her Russian was very good and she was prepared to answer their questions. These were difficult years for Manya, but she became friends with another student at the school and this friendship was a comfort to her.

Kazia Przyborowska was the daughter of a librarian who worked for a noted Polish family. The Przyborowska family lived in Count Zamoyski's Blue Palace and each morning Manya and Kazia met by the Palace gates and walked to school, sometimes cutting through a beautiful park called the Saxon Gardens. Often after school, Manya

The Saxon Gardens of Warsaw, Poland. (Library of Congress)

was invited to Kazia's house, where they sipped lemonade or tea. Manya enjoyed these quiet times away from her home.

Manya attended the government school until she was fifteen, when she graduated first in her class and won a gold medal for being the top student in 1883. Officially, Manya had completed her education, but she wanted to study at a university. However, few universities even outside of Poland accepted female students. Her sister Bronya also wanted to further her education, but first they would have to work and save their money.

Manya, however, was not ready to find work. She had a sensitive and nervous disposition, and at times became depressed. Her father realized that his youngest daughter needed a change of scenery and some fun before she made her way in the world. He decided to send her to a relative's country manor in the south of Poland. Manya spent a peaceful year reading books, playing tag and shuttlecock, gathering strawberries, and having interesting conversations with her educated uncles and cousins. Manya wrote to her friend Kazia, "There are always a great many people, and a freedom, equality and independence such as you can hardly imagine."

One of Manya's favorite memories of her year in the country was the "kulig," a Polish tradition that began with sleighs full of happy young people wearing colorful skirts, beaded vests, red and white pants, and full-sleeved blouses. Stopping from house to house, they were served hot bowls of stew, cakes, doughnuts, red wine, and vodka.

The Polish countryside, near where Manya vacationed. (Library of Congress)

Fiddlers played music and dancers twirled around the floor. Then it was on to another house and more eating and dancing, until they danced the last mazurka at dawn. Manya wrote to Kazia, "I have been to a kulig. You can't imagine how delightful it is, especially when the clothes are beautiful and the boys are well dressed. My costume was very pretty."

As Manya's year of fun came to an end, another invitation arrived for Manya and her sister. They were invited to visit a friend of their mother's at her summer estate near the Carpathian Mountains. It was a magical summer for the sisters. When Manya returned to the family's apartment on Nowolipki Street, she was sixteen. She began to think about getting a teaching or tutoring position. Bronya was already working as a tutor. Until they could afford to go to a real university, the sisters continued their education by attending classes at a forbidden school for girls in Warsaw called the Floating University. The classes had been started by Polish educators and were held at many different places in order to escape detection by the Russian police. It was at this illegal school that Manya developed an interest in science and mathematics.

two
FINDING
A WAY

Manya was taking a risk attending the Floating University. If discovered, she could be punished by the Russian authorities. But she and the other students believed that by continuing their education they could someday free themselves from Russian dominance. This form of intellectual rebellion was called positivism, a philosophy that advocated using education to improve society. Positivists also encouraged educational methods that could be proven to work by empirical observation and offered non-violent ways to protest foreign control over their lives.

In addition to attending classes at the Floating University, Manya and Bronya found work tutoring. Sometimes students came to the Sklodowski home, but often the sisters had to walk long distances to their pupils' houses. The sisters spent hours preparing and teaching the lessons, but could not earn enough for both of them to attend a university.

Bronya decided to attend the University of Paris, also called La Sorbonne. It was one of the most highly regarded institutions of higher learning in Europe, and some female students were welcomed. Bronya had managed to save just enough money for a train ticket to Paris and a single year of tuition. She would need five years of tuition money in order to complete her studies. Manya suggested another way: if they formed a partnership, maybe they could reach their goals sooner. Manya proposed that Bronya begin her medical studies with the money she had saved. Manya, meanwhile, would find a well-paying job as a governess and would send part of her earnings to Bronya and set aside a small amount for her own education. Their father offered to help Bronya with her expenses. Manya ended by saying, "When you are a doctor it will be my turn to go. And then you will help me." At first, Bronya objected. It seemed unfair that she should go first when Manya was the more gifted student, but Manya's mind was made up. Bronya was older and had long dreamed of becoming a doctor.

Manya was seventeen years old in 1885 when she walked into an employment agency. Her fair skin, curly blond hair, and gray eyes stood out against the simple, dark dress she wore to the appointment. She sat quietly in front of the interviewer until the woman began to speak.

"What is your business, mademoiselle? You have references? You have a perfect command of German, Russian, French, Polish, and English? And how much money do you require? But how old are you by the way?"

This picture of Manya was taken the year before she applied for a governess position. (Courtesy of the Association Curie et Joliot-Curie, Paris.)

Manya answered all of the questions, explaining that she spoke "English not so well as the others...." She asked for four hundred rubles a year and a room and meals, and added that she would soon be eighteen. The interviewer wrote on Manya's application: Marya Sklodowska, good references, capable, wants place as governess. Salary: four hundred rubles a year.

Manya went to work for a wealthy Polish family in Warsaw in the winter of 1885. It was not a happy experience. Manya thought the family was insincere and haughty and wasted money on the trappings of wealth while underpaying their servants. In return, Manya's employers thought she was too proud to be a suitable governess. The lady of the house and Manya did not get along, and after three months Manya left. She wrote in her notebook, "One must not enter into contact with people who have been demoralized by wealth . . . I could not endure it any longer."

Manya heard of another governess position in the province of Szczuki, about fifty miles north of Warsaw. Even though this job was farther from home, Manya accepted it because it paid five hundred rubles a year. On January 1, 1886, she said a tearful goodbye to her father and boarded a railway carriage for the long trip to her new employers, the Zorawski family. She arrived eight hours later, having transferred from a railroad car to a sleigh that drove her through the snowy countryside. The journey ended at a large sugar beet farm and processing factory the Zorawskis managed.

Manya was welcomed warmly by the Zorawskis and their daughters. Bronka was eighteen, the same age as Manya; her sister Andzia was ten. The younger siblings were a three-year-old boy named Stas and a six-month-old girl, Maryshna. Three older boys were away at school.

Manya's second governess job got off to a better start than the first one, although the situation was not ideal. In February she wrote a letter to her cousin Henrietta saying that she and the eldest daughter Bronka had become friends, and that the Zorawskis were excellent people. Three months later she wrote to her brother Joseph that Bronka was a good and willing student, but that the younger girl, Andzia, did not have a good memory. It was often a struggle to teach her. Manya took personal responsibility for Andzia's slow progress.

Manya was dismayed by the terrible living and working conditions of the beet workers at the factory. Many of the workers' children were poorly clothed and had no shoes, even in the long, cold winters. She wished she could buy them better clothing and put shoes on their feet, but could not afford to buy new clothes for herself. Manya looked for another way to help. The village schools taught students to read and write Russian, but the parents wanted them to learn in Polish. Keeping their children out of school was their way of rebelling against Russian authority and control. Manya asked her employers if she could instruct the factory workers' children in Polish during her free time. The Zorawski family gave their permission, even though they knew they could be punished by the Russian authorities. Fortunately, the isolation of their country home made this unlikely. Madame Zorawski even permitted her daughter Bronka to assist Manya. Working around a kitchen table in the evenings, the two young women taught Polish to twenty shy but eager students.

Manya's days at her new position were busy. After completing her daily tasks as governess and teacher, she studied physics, chemistry, mathematics, and literature. She was allowed use of the factory library where a chemist, noticing

Manya's interest in science, gave her free chemistry lessons. Manya wanted to perform experiments, but without a laboratory, she had to obtain most of her knowledge of chemistry and physics from books.

At the time, it was unclear whether Manya would ever have a chance to work in a laboratory, or to study at the University of Paris. Nevertheless, she kept to her plan of sending money to Bronya while saving a little for her own education. For the time being she had to be content with her governess job, her students, her independent studies, and her goal of one day earning a college degree. But in the spring of 1886, Manya's private world changed. The Zorawski's eldest son, Kazimierz, came home on vacation from the University of Warsaw.

Kazimierz was an engineering student. At nineteen, he was a year older than Manya. He took notice of the pretty, petite girl with blonde curls who liked to dance and ice skate, but who also had a serious side to her personality. Manya was drawn to Kazimierz's easygoing nature, his good looks, and his interest in mathematics and science. Soon, the young couple began to talk about a future together. Late that summer, Kazimierz asked his parents for permission to marry Manya. The Zorawskis flew into a rage. They were appalled that their son would consider marrying a penniless governess. At first Kazimierz protested his parents' decision, but soon realized that he would lose their financial support if he rebelled and married Manya.

By turns surprised, upset, and embarrassed, Manya reeled at the rejection. Soon, however, she collected herself and

Her on-and-off relationship with Kazimierz Zorawski held Manya back from other personal and professional plans for four years. (Courtesy of the Association Curie et Joliot-Curie, Paris.)

wrote to her cousin Henrietta in December 1887: "Don't believe the report of my approaching marriage; it is unfounded. This tale has been spread about the countryside and even at Warsaw; and though this is not my fault, I am afraid it may bring me trouble."

The easy working relationship Manya had formed with the Zorawski family ended. She wanted to leave, but had promised to help Bronya complete her medical studies. Manya's future was uncertain, but she knew she needed to escape her unpleasant situation.

Manya received good news from her family in 1888. Her father had secured a position as director of a reform school. Not only would his salary increase, he would also receive a comfortable pension for his retirement. Bronya sent word from Paris that she would soon take her medical examinations. Bronya also announced she had met a Polish doctor, Casimir Dluski, and the two were planning to marry. Bronya asked her father to start setting money aside for Manya's education. Manya gave notice to the Zorawski family and left, she said, "with my head high."

When she returned to Warsaw in 1889, Manya accepted another teaching position with a local family. She joined them at a resort beside the Baltic Sea where they were staying for the summer, and continued to work for them when they returned to Warsaw in the fall. Another year passed. And then one day the postman brought a letter from Bronya. The words jumped off the page as she read: "And now you, my little Manya: you must make something of your life sometime. If you can get together a few hundred rubles this year you can come to Paris next year and live with us, where you will find board and lodging."

Manya had been waiting years for this letter. Her dreams of an education were at last coming true. However, she had promised her father that she would return home and they would live together. She also wanted to help her sister Hela, who was depressed following a broken engagement, and there was her brother Joseph to consider. He needed support in his personal life and career. What did it matter

if she denied her own needs for a little longer? Manya
wrote to Bronya:

> I have been stupid, I am stupid, and I shall remain
> stupid all the days of my life, or rather, to translate
> into the style: I have never been, am not, and shall
> never be lucky. I dreamed of Paris as of redemption,
> but the hope of going there left me a long time ago.
> And now that the possibility is offered me, I do not
> know what to do…

Bronya objected to Manya's indecision and the two sisters
worked out a plan. Manya would continue her governess job
until her services were no longer needed. Then she could
share an apartment with her father and sister Hela and,
perhaps, begin tutoring students once more. When Manya
had saved more money and fulfilled her family obligations,
she would leave for Paris, hopefully in two years.

When Manya's governess job ended, she found work
teaching and again resumed her classes at the Floating University. To her delight, she finally got the chance to work
in a chemistry laboratory. Manya's cousin had just returned
from Russia, where he had studied with a Russian chemist
named Dimitri Mendeleyev. Mendeleyev was known for
organizing the elements into a "periodic table" according
to their atomic weights. Manya's cousin was director of the
Museum of Industry and Agriculture in Warsaw, and he
permitted her to conduct science experiments there. This
almost certainly influenced her decision to concentrate her
studies in the fields of chemistry and physics.

In the summer of 1891, Manya traveled to a resort in the Tatra Mountains. Kazimierz Zorawski, her suitor two years earlier, met her there to talk about renewing the relationship, but the two young people still could not find a solution to their problem. Manya made a final break with

THE PERIODIC TABLE OF ELEMENTS

By the early nineteenth century most scientists believed that each element was made up of a different kind of unique atom, and what differentiated atoms was their weight. The scientists reached a baseline for determining atomic weight by comparing it with an atom of hydrogen, the lightest known element.

In 1869, a Russian chemist named Dimitri Mendeleyev began to arrange the sixty-three known elements into a periodic table according to their atomic weights. He organized the elements into horizontal rows, periods, and vertical columns called groups. Elements with similar properties were grouped together. Mendeleyev left blank spaces for elements that he thought must exist but had not yet been discovered.

Although Mendeleyev's periodic table was accepted as a valuable reference source, there were problems with his atomic weight listings. In 1913, British physicist Henry Moseley found that the chemical properties of elements were related more to their atomic numbers than to their atomic weights. The atomic number is the number of protons in the nucleus of each atom. The elements were then rearranged in the periodic table according to their atomic number, along with their chemical symbol.

Today, there are 111 elements listed in The Periodic Table of Elements.

Manya stands behind her father, with Bronya and Hela on the right, in this photograph from 1890. (Courtesy of the Association Curie et Joliot-Curie, Paris.)

Kazimierz, telling him, "If you can't see a way to clear up our situation it is not for me to teach it to you." She returned to Warsaw and wrote to Bronya:

Now Bronya, I ask you for a definite answer. Decide if you can really take me in at your house, for I can come now. I have enough to pay all my expenses. If, therefore, without depriving yourself of a great deal, you could give me my food, write to me, and say so. It would be a great happiness, as that would restore me spiritually after the cruel trials I have been through this summer, which will have an influence on my whole life—but on the other hand I do not wish to impose myself on you.

Manya waited for Bronya's answer. She was twenty-four years old and had waited eight years for the chance to go to Paris. Bronya responded that she should come as soon as possible. Manya wrote that she was "so nervous at the prospect of my departure that I can't speak of anything else." But even so, she had decided that "nothing in life is to be feared. It is only to be understood." With that, Manya said goodbye to her father and siblings and boarded a train headed for Paris.

three
THE HEROIC PERIOD

It took four days to make the one-thousand-mile trip from Warsaw to Paris. Manya traveled fourth class to save money, which meant she did not have a bed, and had to carry her own food and a small stool to sit on. She arrived in Paris in November 1891 exhausted and with little money. But she did have a working command of the French language and a ravenous appetite for knowledge.

Manya's new brother-in-law, Casimir Dluski, met her at the train station. They traveled to the working-class neighborhood of La Vilette by carriage. The Dluskis lived in a small second-floor apartment. Casimir and Bronya were both doctors and their cramped living quarters served as an office during the day.

In her first week, Manya went to the University of Paris to register for classes at the Faculty of Science. On

Marie journeyed from Warsaw to Paris. On this 1911 map, Poland is part of Russia. (University of Texas, Austin)

the registration forms, she signed her name as Marie, the French equivalent of Marya, her Polish given name. From then on, she would be known as Marie to her teachers and colleagues, although her close friends and family continued to call her by her Polish nickname.

The University of Paris, also called La Sorbonne, was founded in the mid 1200s by Robert de Sorbon, a chaplain to Louis IX of France, for the education of theology students. By the late 1800s, La Sorbonne offered education in a variety of fields. The school was also renovating its old buildings, and providing new and fully equipped laboratories for its teachers and students. It was one of the few European universities that accepted female students, although only a few. At the time Marie registered in 1891, La Sorbonne had some two thousand students enrolled in its School of Sciences. Of these, only twenty-three were women.

Intelligent, well-read, and possessing an excellent memory, Marie nevertheless was weak in several subjects, particularly mathematics. She could speak French fairly well, but was unaccustomed to reading, writing, and listening to lectures in French and had to work to improve her language skills.

Founded in 1257, La Sorbonne has a rich history. This image from the 1600s shows the college looking much as it has from its inception to the present day. (Bibliothèque nationale de France, Paris)

Once classes began, Marie rode the omnibus to the campus, an hour trip each way. At the end of the day she returned to the Dluskis' apartment to study in her little room. Her brother-in-law often had his Polish friends over for tea and noisy discussions about Poland's political future. Marie was accustomed to distractions and was able to ignore most interruptions, but she liked Casimir's group of friends and was encouraged to become a part of the warm circle. Marie also liked to attend concerts and other events with her brother-in-law and sister. When she wrote to her father about her social life, he replied that it was not a good idea to spend time in frivolous pursuits, and asked if she had forgotten why she had moved to Paris.

Marie knew her father was right. She decided to move out of her sister's apartment and into a rented room at 3 rue Flatters in the Latin Quarter. The room was close to La Sorbonne. Marie could walk to her classes and save money on carriage fare. She would also have privacy and quiet. Bronya and Casimir helped her move into the tiny attic room. This move was the beginning of the time in Marie's life that her brother-in-law would later call "the heroic period."

Marie survived on the forty Polish rubles a month her father sent. This modest sum had to pay for rent, food, books, paper, medicine, clothing, and any other necessary items. Her room had no running water, and her only source of heat was a small stove she lit only when she had enough money to buy a sack of coal. She slept on a folding bed, boiled water on the small stove, and washed her face and hands from a bowl of cold water. Her closet was a trunk she had brought from Poland. She lived mainly on tea and bread, and ate eggs when she had money to spare. Often, she forgot to eat because she was so wrapped up in her studies. On cold nights, after the university library closed, she came back to her little room and bundled up in layers of clothing to keep warm.

The attic room at 3 rue Flatters was the first of several rooms Marie lived in during her student years. In each, she maintained a simple, monastic life of complete devotion to her studies. Marie wrote to her brother Joseph that she was "working a thousand times as hard as at the beginning of my stay."

The poverty and long hours began to take a toll on her health. The once robust, red-cheeked girl became pale and thin. Her clothes hung loose and the healthy glow disappeared from her face. One day Marie fainted, and Bronya and Casimir were called. They took her to their apartment and diagnosed her condition as malnutrition and fatigue. Bronya fed her soup, beef, potatoes, and vegetables and Marie was soon feeling better. When she had regained her strength, she returned to the attic room and once again put all of her energies into her studies.

In later years, after she became famous, newspaper reporters often portrayed her as a sorrowful woman who was willing to isolate herself in order to concentrate on her work. Marie took a more philosophical attitude, writing in her *Autobiographical Notes*, "Life is not easy for any of us.

But what of that? We must have perseverance and above all confidence in ourselves. We must believe that we are gifted for something and that this thing must be attained."

Marie did not consider it a sacrifice to devote so much of her time and energy to her work. "All that I saw and learned was a new delight to me. It was like a new world opened to me, the world of science, which I was at last permitted to know in all liberty."

Despite her hard work, Marie was nervous at examination time. In July 1893, she took her place in the examination hall and had to force herself to calm down and focus on the test. It took several days for the results to be announced. When the grades were read aloud, Marie's name was the first one on the list. She had graduated with top honors in her class.

With her master's degree in physics in hand, Marie returned to Poland. She planned to spend the summer with her father in Warsaw, but wanted to return to Paris in the fall to study for a second master's degree in mathematics. But there was little money. Again, help arrived, this time through a friend and fellow student, Jadwiga Dydynska, who recommended Marie for the "Alexandrovitch Scholarship," which was offered each year to one deserving Polish student studying abroad. Marie was awarded the scholarship of six hundred rubles, enough money to finance her studies at the University of Paris for another fifteen months.

Marie was now twenty-six years old. After spending August 1893 visiting family and friends, she returned

This photo from Marie's student days was taken on Bronya's balcony, not long after Marie arrived in Paris. (Courtesy of the Association Curie et Joliot-Curie, Paris.)

to Paris, found another small room, and began to work towards a second master's degree. She lived alone, but the solitary life suited her. She wrote, "When one is young and solitary and swallowed up in study, one can 'not have enough to live on'—and yet live to the fullest."

Marie's daily schedule was hectic. After a few hours of sleep, she had a cup of tea or chocolate and, if she could afford it, some bread from a bakery, before hurrying to school. Her physics professor, Gabriel Lippmann, was her favorite. He arranged for the Society for the Encouragement of National Industry to pay Marie to conduct scientific research. Her assignment was to study and measure the magnetic properties of various types of steel. The job paid six hundred francs, which she dearly needed.

Professor Gabriel Lippmann. (Library of Congress)

Marie set up equipment in Professor Lippmann's laboratory at La Sorbonne, but the space was small and the equipment was hard to maneuver. She worried she would not be able to complete her project without a proper laboratory. Once again, a friend stepped in to help. Joseph Kowalski, a Polish professor of physics, told Marie he knew someone who worked at the School of Industrial Physics and Chemistry of the City of Paris (EPCI) who was also doing research on magnetism. He suggested that this well-known French physicist, Pierre Curie, might be able to help her. Professor Kowalski invited Marie to his boarding house for tea so that the two could meet.

Years later, Marie looked back on the spring day in 1894 when she met Pierre Curie:

> Upon entering the room I perceived, standing framed by the French window opening on the balcony, a tall young man with auburn hair and large, limpid eyes. I noticed the grave and gentle expression of his face, as well as a certain abandon in his attitude, suggesting the dreamer absorbed in his reflections. He showed me a simple cordiality and seemed to me very sympathetic.

The two of them discussed scientific and social topics, and discovered they held similar opinions. Pierre asked to see Marie again, and she agreed.

four
MARIE AND PIERRE

From their correspondence, it appears Pierre was convinced he wanted to marry Marie soon after meeting her. Marie, on the other hand, was not initially interested in developing a romantic relationship. She liked and respected the soft-spoken older man, but her focus was on earning her degrees and returning to Poland.

Pierre and his brother Jacques had both shown an early interest in nature and science. They were encouraged by their parents, Dr. Eugene Curie and Sophie Curie. Pierre's early education was closely monitored by his parents, who were afraid their younger son was a daydreamer and easily distracted. He was slow to read and write, but could grasp complex mathematical ideas early. His parents taught him at home and Dr. Curie took Pierre on field trips to study the natural world up close. When Pierre was a teenager, his father hired a tutor, Professor Albert Bazille, to teach him mathematics and Latin. This more informal method of instruction suited Pierre's temperament, and at age sixteen he earned a bachelor of science degree. He then attended La Sorbonne and earned a master's degree in physics by the age of eighteen.

When Marie met Pierre, he was an established physics teacher and laboratory chief at the School of Industrial Physics and Chemistry of the City of Paris. His research was on the structure and properties of crystals, a science called crystallography. When he was twenty-one, he and Jacques had discovered that applying pressure to crystals produced an electric current. The brothers invented an instrument that they called a piezo-quartz electrometer to measure the faint current. Pierre and Jacques wrote ten research papers on what they called "piezoelectricity," from the Greek word *piezein*, to press tightly. The brothers were also authorities on electromagnetism.

Pierre was shy and uncomfortable in the company of women. At twenty-two he wrote, "Women…draw us away from dedication….Women of genius are rare." At thirty-five he still lived at home with his parents. When he met Marie in 1894, Pierre had been teaching and working in physics for about fifteen years and must have been surprised to find how much he had in common with the Polish student nine years his junior. Both were gentle and quiet, devoted to work, inclined to keep journals, and attached to close and loving families. Education was important in both families; Pierre's father and older brother were both doctors.

Pierre Curie, as he looked a few years after his marriage. (Courtesy of the Granger Collection.)

Although Pierre had no laboratory space to offer Marie, he was generous with his advice and assistance. He gave

Marie a copy of his 1894 paper, "Symmetry in Physical Phenomena" inscribed, "To Mlle Sklodowska, with the respect and friendship of the author."

Marie and Pierre spent time together that spring. Sometimes they sat at the small table in her attic room, drinking tea and discussing scientific matters. Other times they walked along the Paris streets and stopped in coffee shops. Pierre told her about his family's home in Sceaux, located seven miles from La Sorbonne. Marie told him that she was planning to return to Warsaw to see her family and visit the countryside she loved so much. Pierre said he also enjoyed the outdoors, but grew nervous when she talked of leaving Paris. He asked, "But you're coming back in October? Promise me that you will come back! If you stay in Poland, you can't possibly continue your studies. You have no right to abandon science now...."

Marie said she would probably return after a short visit. Pierre urged her to think of a future together, but Marie considered herself duty-bound to return to Poland. Pierre offered to go with her, but Marie left alone, without making any promises. She traveled to Switzerland and then to Poland with her father. Pierre wrote Marie many letters, always urging her to return to France. On August 10, 1894, he wrote:

> I hope you are laying up a stock of good air and that you will come back to us in October. As for me, I think I shall not go anywhere; I shall stay in the country, where I spend the whole day in front of my open window or in the garden.

Then in early September, he wrote:

> . . . As you may imagine, your letter worries me. I strongly advise you to come back to Paris in October. It would be a great grief to me if you did not come back this year: but it is not out of a friend's selfishness that I tell you to come back. Only, I believe that you would work better here and can do a more solid and useful job.

Two weeks later, Pierre wrote:

> Your letter worried me a great deal; I felt that you were worried and undecided. Your letter from Warsaw reassures me a little; I feel you have regained your calm. Your picture pleases me enormously. How kind of you to send it to me! I thank you with all my heart.

Marie returned to Paris in October. Her sister Bronya offered her a room next to her medical practice. Marie was at school all day while Bronya saw patients, and at night it was quiet and Marie was able to study and sleep without any interruptions or distractions.

Both Marie and Pierre were busy with their research, but often saw each other. Pierre had a difficult time concentrating on his work because he was so preoccupied with trying to persuade Marie to marry him. He appealed to Bronya to argue his case for him. He even invited Bronya to come with him and Marie when they visited his parents. Pierre's mother took Bronya aside and asked her to talk to Marie about her son. She told Bronya, "There isn't a soul on earth to equal my Pierre. Don't let your sister hesitate. She will be happier with him than with anybody."

Yet Marie did hesitate. It took her almost a year to say yes to Pierre's proposal. She wrote to her childhood friend Kazia about her decision:

> When you receive this letter our Manya will have changed her name. I am about to marry the man I told you about last year in Warsaw. It is a sorrow to me to have to stay forever in Paris, but what am I to do? Fate has made us deeply attached to each other and we cannot endure the idea of separating.

On July 26, 1895, Marie and Pierre were married at City Hall. His family hosted a small reception in the garden of their home in Sceaux. Marie wore a dress given to her by Bronya's husband's mother. Marie's family traveled from Poland for the happy occasion. On that day, she became know as Madame Marie Curie. The next day the couple began their honeymoon on two new bicycles they bought with money given to them as a wedding present.

Marie and Pierre enjoyed riding bicycles, which in the late 1800s was a popular activity. From its early stages as a contraption with high wheels, the bicycle had been rede-signed. The new models featured smaller wheels, air-filled tires, and brakes. Bicycling was an activity both men and women could enjoy. For Marie, it was a way to spend time

Pierre and Marie pose with their new top-of-the-line bicycles and cycling outfits.
(Courtesy of the Association Curie et Joliot-Curie, Paris.)

with her husband, to ride through the countryside that she loved, and to enjoy the fresh air outside of Paris.

The day after their wedding, Marie and Pierre set out to explore the French countryside and back roads. They rode along the coastline of Brittany and explored the Auvergne Mountains of south-central France. Later in their marriage, they often rode their bicycles to visit Pierre's family in Sceaux. They also took their bikes with them on trains when they made longer trips.

On returning from their honeymoon, Marie and Pierre moved into a small three-room apartment near

The Curies, in their first year of marriage. (Courtesy of the Association Curie et Joliot-Curie, Paris.)

La Sorbonne. Marie chose it because it overlooked a garden and sunshine lit the rooms. She was not particularly interested in decorating the apartment, and Pierre was not concerned with comfortable surroundings. Their furnishings were limited to a bed, table, chairs, some lighting, a stove, and other basic necessities. Marie splurged only on fresh flowers, which she placed in each room. She had never taken an interest in cooking or any other domestic skills. Her life had been that of a governess, a student, and a research scientist. Now her responsibilities included those of a wife, and she began to teach herself to cook inexpensive and nourishing meals, to take care of two sets of clothing, to keep the apartment clean, and to manage the family's budget. Pierre earned only five hundred francs a month from his teaching, and Marie was still studying to become a teacher. She had learned how to be careful with her money as a student living on practically nothing, and now she began recording household and personal expenses in small notebooks.

Marie's days began early. She walked to the market and often peeled vegetables for lunch before she left for class. She then walked to La Sorbonne to attend lectures, and later, to the laboratory. In the evening, she and Pierre returned home and she prepared dinner. It was a point of pride for Marie to learn to cook in the French style. She pored over her cookbook, noting her successes and failures in the margins. When the dishes had been cleared, she studied at the small kitchen table

The left bank of the Seine, close to La Sorbonne, in the heart of Paris. Marie would have seen a similar bustle on her daily walks to market and school. (Library of Congress)

before going to bed. Combining a career and a personal life was a challenge for Marie, but she was determined to continue her research.

In November 1895, Marie wrote to her brother Joseph about her life with Pierre.

> . . . Everything goes well with us; we are both healthy and life is kind to us. I am arranging my flat little by little, but I intend to keep it to a style which will give me no worries and will not require attention, as I have very little help: a woman who comes for an hour a

day to wash the dishes and do the heavy work. I do the cooking and housekeeping myself.

Marie's life grew more complicated when she became pregnant with her first child. It was a difficult pregnancy and she was often ill and found it difficult to work. In addition, Pierre's mother had developed breast cancer, and he was helping with her care.

In July, Marie left Paris for a rest near the Brittany seacoast in a small town called Port-Blanc. Later, her father and a friend joined her. Pierre visited her when he could get away from work, and he wrote letters to her whenever they were separated. Pierre was at loose ends without Marie. He wrote, "My little girl, so dear, so sweet, whom I love so much, I had your letter today and was very happy....Nothing new here, except that I miss you very much: my soul flew away with you..." He wrote in Polish, which he learned to please his new wife.

Marie returned to Paris after a restful summer. On September 12, 1897, her first child, a girl, was delivered by her father-in-law, Dr. Eugene Curie. Marie and Pierre named her Irene. Marie began a journal describing her baby's size, growth, health, and important events such as Irene's first tooth, first steps, and first words.

This happy event was followed only two weeks later by the death of Pierre's mother. Irene would never know her paternal grandmother, but she formed a close attachment to Pierre's father when Dr. Curie moved in with the young family. He and a nurse attended to the baby while Marie studied and worked. This arrangement helped Marie manage her workload while caring for a young family. The overwork had already plunged her into depression. But now she had time to return to her study of the quickly changing world of physical science.

five
RADIATION

After Marie earned her teaching diploma and finished her research on tempered steels, she needed to find a research subject suitable for graduate work. She was still determined to earn her doctorate.

Marie and Pierre both were always in need of good laboratory space and equipment. She recalled years later, in her *Autobiographical Notes*, something Pierre had written to his director in 1903 after he had been awarded a decoration by the Legion d'Honneur. Pierre refused the tribute by saying, "I pray you to thank the Minister, and to inform him that I do not in the least feel the need of a decoration, but that I do feel the greatest need for a laboratory."

Marie knew she was not entitled to a laboratory because she had not yet earned the proper credentials. She also knew that her low status as a woman in the scientific community worked against her. Yet even Pierre, who had proven himself an exceptional physicist, had to take whatever work space the School of Physics offered.

Her doctoral work would require some sort of laboratory, however. Finally, the director of the School of Physics where Pierre taught offered her the use of a small, unheated storage space in the school's building. The room was dreary, but it was furnished with a blackboard, some wooden tables and a chair, and laboratory equipment. Best of all, Pierre was close at hand.

The rough shed where Marie and Pierre did their groundbreaking work on radioactive elements. (Courtesy of the Association Curie et Joliot-Curie, Paris.)

Henri Becquerel came from a distinguished line of scientists. He shared the 1903 Nobel Prize in Physics with the Curies for his discovery of spontaneous radioactivity. A unit of radioactivity and two craters on the moon are named for him. (Library of Congress)

Marie could now select a topic. While looking over scientific journals and other reports on experiments, she read a paper written by a physicist named Henri Becquerel, the son of a well-known scientist. Becquerel had become interested, as had many other researchers, in the recent discovery made by a German named Wilhelm Conrad Röntgen.

Röntgen, a professor at the University of Wurzburg, stumbled upon the discovery of X-rays by accident. He was working on cathode rays, which are produced when an electric current flows through a vacuum tube. Röntgen and others knew that cathode rays moved slower than light and could be diverted by a magnetic field, but no one knew exactly what the rays were and where they came from. In his experiment, Röntgen was simply trying to find out if the particles in cathode rays penetrated the glass tube. He did this by covering a vacuum tube with black paper so it would be possible to detect the rays as they escaped the tube.

Röntgen donated all of his Nobel Prize money to his university and refused to patent the discovery. Although other scientists began calling his discovery Röntgen rays, he always preferred the name X-ray. (Library of Congress)

When Röntgen conducted his experiment on November 8, 1895, he noticed that a nearby paper screen that had been painted with a phosphorescent chemical glowed when the current passed through the vacuum tube, which was completely covered by the black paper. The rays were not only escaping the tube—they were also penetrating the paper covering, striking the screen, and leaving an impression.

Excited by his accidental discovery, Röntgen conducted more experiments using photographic plates instead of treated paper. This way he could have permanent images of the interior of the objects he sent the rays through. He began shooting the rays through a box with coins inside and capturing the image of the coins. In an experiment that became famous throughout the world, he directed the rays at his wife's hand, which was placed on a photographic plate. When he was finished he had a clear image of the bones in her hand. When published, evidence of how the new discovery could be used in medicine created a sensation. Röntgen named this new phenomenon X-rays, because X is the mathematical symbol for an unknown quantity. For his discovery, Röntgen was awarded the first-ever Nobel Prize in Physics in 1901.

Within weeks after the announcement of Röntgen's sensational discovery, dozens of scientists were studying X-rays. Becquerel's first step was to duplicate Röntgen's experiments. Then he tried to determine if X-rays could be produced without a vacuum tube by using phosphorescent materials instead. He first placed

one type of phosphorescent material, radium salts, on photographic paper and left it in the sunlight. He thought the light would be needed to activate the X-rays.

After succeeding in producing a X-ray image of the radium salts with light, Becquerel decided to repeat the

J. J. THOMSON AND SUBATOMIC CORPUSCLES

J. J. Thomson, a researcher at the Cavendish Laboratory at Cambridge University in Great Britain, was the first to suggest cathode rays were actually small particles escaping from an atom. He tested this hypothesis by conducting three experiments.

It had earlier been discovered that the cathode rays carried an electric charge. Thomson's first experiment determined that the charge can not be separated from the ray. In the second experiment, he proved that the rays do bend when moved through a magnetic field. Thomson concluded this meant that cathode rays are charges of negative electricity carried by particles of matter.

One huge question remained: what were these particles of matter? Were they atoms, or were they smaller than atoms? For years it had been assumed that the atom was indivisible, the smallest particle in nature. However, Thomson did not think the amount of charge carried by the particles was strong enough to be carried by an atom.

Thomson's next experiment attempted to measure the ratio of charge to mass, called the *mle*. Because he could not directly measure the mass or electric charge of such a small particle, he measured how much the rays were bent by a magnetic field, to determine its mass, and the strength of the energy in the ray, in order to calculate the *mle*. This third experiment proved that the

mass to electric charge ratio was more than a thousand times smaller than the *mle* of a single atom of charged hydrogen. This could mean that the mass of the particle was either very small, or the electric charge was very large, or some combination. However, it was more likely the mass and charge were smaller, because the particle was smaller than an atom.

Thomson announced his results in a lecture delivered on April 30, 1897, at the Royal Institution in London. In the address he stated that cathode rays are charged particles, which he called corpuscles, and that the corpuscles are part of the atoms, in other words, sub-atomical. Two years later, in 1899, Thomson was able to find a value for the mass of the cathode ray particles, which he still called corpuscles. He determined they had approximately one two-thousandth of the mass of a hydrogen atom, and that the particles are "a part of the mass of the atom getting free and becoming detached from the original atom."

Later, a student of Thomson's named Ernest Rutherford built on Thomson's work and suggested an atomic model with a nucleus, positively charged center, and particles that orbited the nucleus much as the planets orbit the sun. The science of nuclear physics was born.

("On the Masses of the Ions in Gases at Low Pressures," J. J. Thomson, Philosophical Magazine, December 1899, Series 5, Vol. 48, No. 295, p. 547)

experiment and to try to capture an image of a copper cross. But the weather was dreary and overcast for several days, and Becquerel wrapped the cross, radium salts, and photographic paper in a black cloth and put it in a drawer. When the weather improved he opened the drawer and discovered, after developing the paper, that a clear image of the cross was evident. Radium salts had produced an X-ray image without being activated by light.

It was Becquerel's report of this experiment that prompted Marie to continue his work. Becquerel had moved on to other projects by then. Her first goal was to measure the strength of Becquerel's rays. She planned to do this by using the piezoquartz electrometer designed by Pierre and his brother, but first it had to be modified to be sensitive enough to measure the very slight current generated by the rays.

One of the first things Marie discovered was that the rays produced by uranium were constant, regardless of the state of the uranium. It did not matter if it was solid or ground up, and the more uranium that was tested, the more intense the rays became. This was an important discovery.

It was what Marie did next that led to her greatest work. She developed a hypothesis that the rays were an atomic property of the uranium. At the time most physicists still thought the atom was the smallest particle in nature. But Marie was speculating that maybe the atom was not the smallest particle in uranium—that X-rays existed because of something built into the atom.

In March 1898 Marie named the phenomenon radioactivity, from the Latin *radius*, meaning ray. She also knew radioactivity was present in both uranium and thorium, and suspected it was present in other yet-undiscovered elements. In the following month she wrote a paper that her professor presented to the Academy of Sciences because women had not yet been allowed to address the organization. The paper foretold the direction her research would be taking:

> ... I then made the hypothesis that the ores of uranium and thorium contain in small quantity a substance much more strongly radioactive than either uranium or thorium itself. This substance could not be one of the known elements, because these had already been examined; it must, therefore, be a new chemical element.

Marie wanted to find these new elements that produced radioactivity. She began to test other compounds with Pierre's help. He offered to postpone his own research on crystals to assist her.

Marie began her research with pitchblende, the raw ore that is left over after uranium and other minerals are extracted. She found that pitchblende was more radioactive than uranium alone. Marie and Pierre reasoned that pitchblende must contain unknown elements that were highly radioactive. Within a short time, Marie discovered traces of a radioactive element four hundred times as active as uranium. She named the new element "polonium" for her homeland. Five months later, she found traces of a second element that registered even higher radiation than polonium. She called this element radium. The Curies collaborated on a paper entitled "On A New Radio-Active Substance Contained in Pitchblende."

Marie knew she would have to isolate both polonium and radium in their pure states and determine their atomic weights before the scientific community would be convinced the powerful radioactive elements existed. But to do this, she and Pierre needed a larger laboratory. By this time their work had attracted notice and the School of Physics offered them the use of an abandoned shed that had once been used by medical students for dissecting cadavers. The shed had a glass-house roof that leaked when it rained. Summers were hot and in the winter, cold drafts blew through the run-down building. Inside were

A scientist separates radium out of pitchblende. (from Marie Curie's *Pierre Curie*)

a few pine tables, gas burners, a cast-iron stove, a blackboard for scribbling notes, a desk, and some laboratory equipment. There was a courtyard beside the shed that could be used for chemical experiments and preparations. They moved in and began working day and night.

Marie's next step was to find a source of pitchblende. She located a uranium plant in St. Joachimsthal, Austria that had ready supplies of pitchblende that it was willing to sell for next to nothing. She described in her *Autobiographical Notes* how she felt when the pitchblende was delivered to the laboratory shed.

> How glad I was when the sacks arrived, with the brown dust mixed with pine needles, and when the activity proved even greater than that of the primitive ore. It was a stroke of luck that the residues had not been thrown far away or disposed of in some way, but left in a heap in the pine wood near the plant.

The next step was the most difficult. Pitchblende comprises twenty to thirty different elements in various combinations. Marie had to sift through all these elements to find the hidden radioactive substances. It was like looking through a haystack for a needle, one straw at a time.

Marie and Pierre worked in the ramshackle laboratory from 1898–1902. Pierre concentrated on determining the properties of polonium and radium, such as their weight, strength, hardness, and density. Marie concentrated on extracting a recognizable form of the two elements from the pitchblende. To separate miniscule amounts of radium and

THE CURIES AND FRACTIONAL CRYSTALLIZATION

Crystals are solid substances composed of closely spaced atoms that arrange in repeating patterns and form a solid. There are seven basic crystal formations: cubic, orthorhombic, hexagonal, tetragonal, trigonal, monoclinic, and triclinic. Gemstones are made up of colorful crystals. Rocks are also crystalline, although they may not look like crystal formations.

The crystallization process separates substances in solid materials. For example, when sugar is boiled and then cooled, a crystalline structure is formed. The type of crystal formed depends on the chemical composition of the fluid and the conditions under which it becomes solid.

When Pierre and Jacques Curie began their study of crystals, it was thought that heat caused complex crystals to become electrically charged by a phenomenon called "pyroelectricity." Their research revealed that the electric charge was not caused by heat but by changes within the crystals when pressure is applied. They developed an instrument called the piezo-quartz electrometer that measured small amounts of electrical charge produced when pressure is exerted on a crystal.

Marie Curie used a technique of chemical analysis called fractional crystallization to purify radium and polonium from a boiling mixture of pitchblende ore. Fractional crystallization causes different substances within the solid material to form crystals at different temperatures. Larger crystals form first, smaller crystals follow, and then the impurities are separated by a filtering process, leaving pure solid crystals.

polonium from the two elements with which they tended to combine—bismuth and barium—she had to stand in the courtyard over large kettles of pitchblende for hours, stirring the mixture with an iron pipe. She later described the separation process: "It was killing work to carry the receivers, to pour off the liquids and to stir, for hours at a stretch, the boiling matter in a smelting basin."

As the mixture cooled, pure crystals were created in the pitchblende, in a process called fractional crystallization. This method refines and purifies substances based on the rates and temperatures at which different substances form crystals. Marie used it to distill the pure minerals. As the final measure of proof that polonium and radium were indeed unique elements, she worked with a colleague to record the spectral light emitted by each substance as it was boiled and converted to gas.

In 1902, Marie was finally able to isolate a small amount of radium salts (radium atoms combined with other types of atoms, producing a white color) that measured 1/50th of a teaspoon. She determined from this small sample that radium's atomic weight was 225. Later she isolated a gram, or 1/4 teaspoon, of radium.

In 1903 Marie published a paper on radium in the journal *Proceedings of Science*. She also successfully presented her doctoral thesis before a science board of her peers that explained the process of isolating and refining radium, and how to determine its atomic weight.

Four years of working with highly radioactive materials permanently altered Marie and Pierre. Unprotected exposure to radiation destroys healthy body cells and tissue. They both had red and irritated skin on their hands and fingers. Marie developed damage to her lungs from breathing toxic chemical fumes and Pierre came down with crippling rheumatism in his legs and back. Both suffered from fatigue due to the combination of long

The Curies in the early 1900s, after several years of prolonged exposure to radiation. (Courtesy of the Association Curie et Joliot-Curie, Paris.)

work hours, poor health, loss of appetite, and lowered red blood cell counts. Once, Pierre purposely exposed his arm to radium, only to see the skin turn red as though it was burned. It took over a month for the sore to heal and, even then, it looked unhealthy. Their colleague Henri Becquerel also suffered radiation burns. In 1901 he told the Curies that he had inadvertently carried a tube of radium in his vest pocket for six hours. Although he felt no pain, a mark the size and shape of the tube appeared fifteen days later.

If Marie and Pierre knew about the damage they were doing to their bodies, they did not mention it. They were absorbed in their work. Marie wrote in her *Autobiographical Notes*:

> One of our joys was to go into our workroom at night; we then perceived on all sides the feebly luminous silhouettes of the bottles or capsules containing our products. It was really a lovely sight and one always new to us. The glowing tubes looked like faint, fairy lights.

The Curies had their work, each other, and their daughter Irene. Pierre had realized his hope of pursuing a scientific life with Marie, but he could not have suspected that their work would bring them so much fame that it would disrupt their beloved experiments.

six
THE PRICE
OF FAME

The first word of their new fame came to the husband and wife team on December 10, 1903, when the Academy of Sciences in Stockholm, Sweden, announced that they were winners of the third Nobel Prize in Physics. Pierre and Marie Curie had to share their prize with Henri Becquerel for the discovery of radioactivity, but it was still a sensation. She was the first woman to win what was already the most famous award in science.

The winners were to receive a gold medal along with a diploma and a cash prize of 70,000 gold francs. The Curies were awarded as a couple, and so they shared their half while Becquerel received the other half. The Academy had been quick to recognize the importance of the discovery of radium, which was already viewed as a potential treatment for cancer and other diseases.

The Curies thanked the Academy publicly, but said they could not travel the forty-hour trip to Stockholm for the award ceremony because of their work schedule and exhaustion. Marie was suffering from nervous exhaustion coupled with depression, brought on by a recent miscarriage.

But Nobel Prize winners were required to give an acceptance speech. After pressure was put on them by Pierre's superiors, they traveled in April 1904, to Stockholm, Sweden, where Pierre gave a speech on "Radioactive Substances, Especially Radium." Marie was seated in the audience instead of beside him on the stage, but Pierre made it very clear that it was Madame Curie who had discovered the radioactive elements of polonium and radium, while he had confined his own research to determining their properties. In his speech, Pierre referred to Madame Curie ten times, modestly downplaying his own contributions.

Marie's absence on the stage is a clear indication of the role women were still relegated to in science and other intellectual activities in the early twentieth century. Although she was primarily responsible for making the discoveries, some members of the Nobel Prize committee had resisted including her in the prize at all, much less letting her share the stage with men.

Women were valued and admired for the roles they played within their families, but they were not admitted into the professions. The most challenging job to which a woman might aspire was a teaching position in a middle school for girls. The very idea of a woman entering the

THE NOBEL PRIZE

Alfred Nobel was born on October 21, 1833, in Stockholm, Sweden. His father was an engineer and inventor. His mother came from a wealthy family. When Alfred was four, he moved with his family to Finland, and later to Russia.

Alfred's father became a successful manufacturer of armaments. He also designed steam engines. He wanted Alfred, who was very intelligent, to become a chemical engineer. Alfred, who could speak several languages by the age of seventeen, developed into a quiet, peaceful man with a talent for invention. He also enjoyed reading poetry and literature. After traveling for some time, Alfred went to work in his father's company and began to experiment with nitroglycerine, a powerful explosive liquid. He soon obtained a patent for a detonator he called the "Nobel lighter."

Alfred Nobel, his father, and a brother returned to Sweden in 1863, where he continued to experiment with nitroglycerine. In 1864, an explosion in his factory killed his brother and other workers. When his brother died, a French newspaper called Nobel a "merchant of death."

Undeterred, Nobel went on to invent dynamite, which could be transported and ignited much more safely than nitroglycerine. Dynamite soon proved to be indispensable to mining and civil engineering. Nobel obtained a patent on dynamite, which quickly earned him a fortune. He also worked on developing other products, such as synthetic rubber and leather. When he died in 1896, he had more than three hundred patents in his name.

Alfred Nobel never married and had no children. He left a will with instructions that "The whole of my remaining realizable estate shall be dealt with in the following way: the capital, invested in safe securities by my executors, shall constitute a fund, the interest on which shall be annually distributed in the form of prizes to those who, during the preceding year shall have conferred the greatest benefit on mankind."

His relatives contested by the will, but it was upheld. It has been speculated that Nobel wanted to be remembered for something other than the invention of dynamite and as a manufacturer of weapons.

On December 10, 1901, the first annual Alfred Nobel Prize awards were presented to people of all races and nationalities who had made significant contributions in physics, chemistry, literature, peace, physiology, and medicine. The category of economics was added in 1969. The first award in physics was given to German physicist Wilhelm Conrad Röntgen for his early work on X-rays. Two years later, Marie and Pierre Curie and Henri Becquerel won the third annual Nobel Prize in Physics for their work on radioactivity. In 1911, Marie was awarded a second Nobel Prize, this one in chemistry, for discovering radium and polonium and isolating radium.

Every year, one hundred to 250 men and women are nominated for the Nobel Prize. There are one to three winners in each category. In the case of multiple winners, the prize money is shared equally. In addition to a large cash prize from the Alfred Nobel Foundation, a diploma of recognition and a gold medal is also awarded.

field of science was peculiar, and the notion that she might compete with her male colleagues was objectionable. That she would win in the race to announce a new discovery was downright offensive to many scientists working in that era.

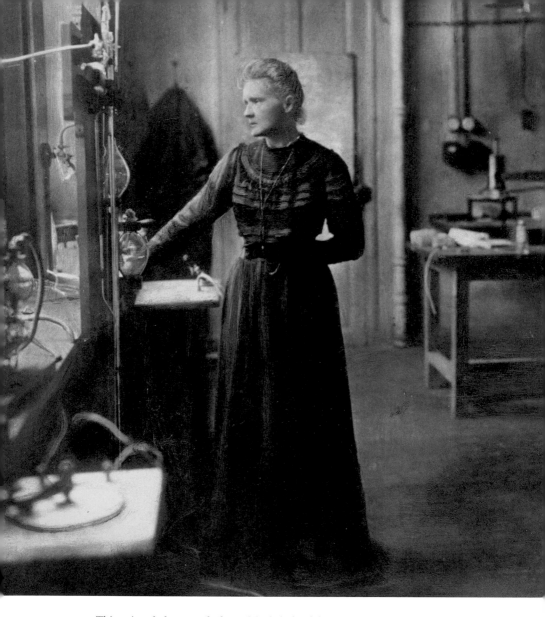

This painted photograph shows Marie in her laboratory. (Courtesy of the Granger Collection.)

Fortunately for Marie, her husband did not share the common opinion. Pierre had stood beside Marie as she worked long hours in their laboratory, repeating experiments over and over again to verify her findings. He had assisted her in calibrating the equipment to measure radiant energy, but he knew that the honors belonged chiefly to her. When the Swedish Academy of Sciences had proposed awarding the Nobel Prize to Pierre and not to Marie, he responded that he would not accept the prize unless Madame Curie was recognized as an equal partner.

Marie and Pierre set aside much of their prize money to purchase new laboratory equipment. They also shared their earnings with family members. Marie's sister, Bronya, had moved with her family to Poland to build a sanitarium, and the Curies contributed to the project. They also used the prize money and later monetary awards to pay for their travel to other countries to receive awards and to speak at scientific conferences.

At these meetings, their failing health was noted by friends and colleagues. In 1903 Marie was pale, thin, and prematurely gray and wrinkled. Pierre, forty-five, suffered from severe pain in his back and legs. Marie urged him to stop teaching and to pay more attention to his health, but they were Nobel Prize winners now, and the demands on their time were greater than ever. There were requests for newspaper and magazine interviews, invitations to lecture, and letters to answer. Marie said of this period, "Our life has been altogether spoiled by honors and fame."

The Curies' main interest was always science. They wanted to advance the techniques for isolating and refining radium. But others were more interested in how to profit from the new discoveries.

At the time, electric power was still in its early stages. New power-driven machinery led to increases in the

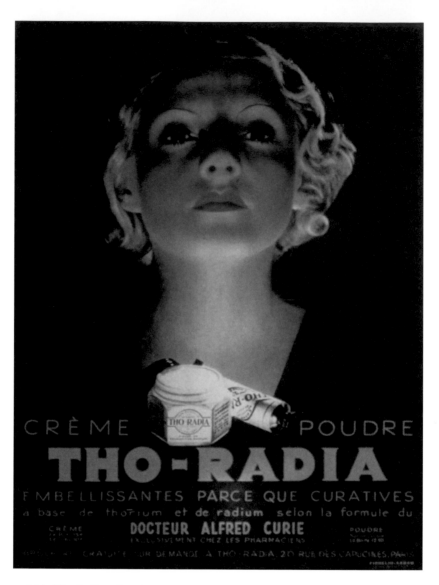

This Tho-Radia advertisement claimed the beauty product possessed curative properties. (Courtesy of the Association Curie et Joliot-Curie, Paris.)

production of metals, ceramics, textiles, farm crops, and many other goods. Science and technology rushed to keep up with the new demands made by economies through-out the industrializing world. Newspapers and magazines capitalized on consumers' preoccupation with all the new developments. Stories about a talented female scientist were sure to make headlines. In addition, articles about and advertisements for personal-use products containing small amounts of radium began to appear. The products ranged from toothpaste and hair-loss solutions to lipsticks and rejuvenating health drinks. No one really knew if radium was really a cure for any medical conditions, but that did not stop thousands from trying to cash in on the exciting new discoveries.

The Curies, along with Becquerel, were cautiously optimistic about the medical value of radiation. Pierre, more than Marie, realized that radium could be a friend or an enemy of humanity. In his Nobel Prize speech he warned that "in the hands of criminals, radium may become very dangerous, and here one may well ask oneself if mankind benefits from knowing the secrets of nature, if we are mature enough to take advantage of them or if this knowledge isn't harmful to us." Yet, in spite of its dangers, radium was welcomed by the general population.

Marie and Pierre might have become wealthy if they had patented the process of extracting and refining radium into its purest state. In 1904, the price of a single gram of radium was 750,000 gold francs (over $110,000 in today's U.S. currency). A patent would have given them exclusive worldwide rights to the manufacture of radium and freed them from financial worries. Instead, the Curies chose to publish papers on their research, sharing their knowledge with the scientific world. However, their decision to forego a patent did not mean they would turn down other monetary offers and awards. Pierre spoke for himself and Marie when he said, "We must make a living, and this forces us to become a wheel in the machine."

The Curies were offered a contract by an entrepreneur named Armet de Lisle. De Lisle proposed to provide them laboratory space in his factory in return for their help in teaching his workers the tedious process of extracting radium from uranium ore. Their joint aim was large-scale manufacture of radium for scientific research and commercial profit. The Curies accepted de Lisle's offer and began receiving royalties, but were still far from wealthy. In addition to her work in the laboratory, Marie taught classes twice a week at a private girls' school at Sevres, outside of Paris, and classes in physics at the University of Paris—another first for a woman. Her schedule was so busy that Marie barely had any time to spend with her seven-year-old daughter, Irene, who was often in the care of a governess or her grandfather.

In April 1904, Marie discovered she was pregnant. Having had an earlier miscarriage, she resolved to take better care of herself and scheduled one of her rare vacations for that summer. She rented a small cottage on the Normandy coast where she could spend time with Irene, and her sisters and friends came to visit them. Marie swam in the ocean, picked flowers in the meadows, and laid a blanket down for picnic lunches with Irene and Pierre. But even in this secluded spot, they were interrupted by reporters and curious people asking questions about their lives and work.

Marie enjoyed her days away from the laboratory, but Pierre seemed unable to relax. Work was never far from his mind. Although he was in poor health, he returned again and again to his study of how radium affects other materials. Marie was also very much involved in discovering new radioactive elements, but she was trying to balance her work with her responsibilities as a mother, and to regain her own health.

On December 6, 1904, a second daughter, Eve Denise, was born. Marie began to take more interest in decorating her home, cooking meals, sewing clothes for the girls, and spending more time with Irene, who found it hard to share her mother's attention with the new baby. The Curies had reached a happy period in their lives together. They shared a loving family and rewarding careers.

The following year, Pierre was offered a teaching job at La Sorbonne. The prestigious position included new laboratory space in Paris. He accepted the offer. Marie became chief of the new laboratory. At last, she had official university rights to work in her husband's laboratory. She was paid 2,400 francs a year.

In April 1906, Marie and her children again left Paris for a vacation in the countryside, this time in St. Remy, an hour away by train. Pierre was too busy with work to accompany them. Marie, with eight-year-old Irene and fourteen-month-old Eve, enjoyed the spring flowers and butterflies, fresh milk from a dairy, and walks through the meadows. Pierre pulled himself away from his laboratory to join them for visits. The photographs taken during this

The French countryside around St. Remy. (Library of Congress)

vacation show a happy, relaxed family, but in reality Pierre was anxious and restless. He told Marie that he wanted to return to Paris ahead of schedule to proceed with his work. Marie persuaded him to stay in the countryside a little longer. He agreed, resting throughout the weekend and departing on Monday, April 16. Marie and the children followed two days later, and on the 18th, she attended a dinner with him.

On Thursday, April 19, the Curie family awoke to a rainy, gloomy day. Marie was preoccupied with helping Irene and Eve with their clothes. She and Pierre exchanged words as he opened his umbrella and hurried off to his laboratory. Later in the day he was hurrying to meet some colleagues for lunch. As he approached the busy intersection of Pont Neuf and rue Dauphine, a tangle of horse-drawn carriages, wagons and pedestrians filled the wet, slippery streets. Instead of waiting for the traffic to thin, Pierre impatiently stepped off the curb into the path of a wagon pulled by two large draft horses. One of the horses crashed into him. Pierre, struggling to regain his balance, grabbed onto the horse's chest to steady himself, but the two animals were now frightened and surged forward. Pierre's legs crumpled beneath him and he fell under the moving wagon. The two front wheels missed him, but the left rear wheel rolled over his head and crushed his skull. Pierre Curie was dead at age forty-nine.

seven
"I WILL TRY"

Pierre's death was a terrible blow to Marie, but she held up, as usual, and faced her responsibilities. She managed to receive the body at home, contact family and friends, and arrange funeral services. It was not until Pierre's brother Jacques arrived that Marie burst into tears.

Pierre Curie was buried in the cemetery at Sceaux beside his mother on April 21, 1906. A newspaper account reported that Marie scattered flowers over the coffin in a slow and determined way while friends and family members watched silently.

At the age of thirty-eight, Marie was a widow. Initially she withdrew, and stayed mostly at home and took care of her children. The tragedy threw her into a deep depression. Her father-in-law was a comforting presence, and she eased her pain by writing in a journal, addressing her late husband directly, "I do not understand that I am to live henceforth without seeing you, without smiling at the sweet companion of my life."

Marie decreed that Pierre's name should never again be spoken in her home. She knew she must continue to

Marie, with daughters Eve and Irene, two years after Pierre's death. (Courtesy of the Association Curie et Joliot-Curie, Paris.)

care for her daughters as well as for herself, even though she no longer felt any joy in life, confiding in her diary she would never again be happy. Photographs taken after Pierre's death show a sad-eyed, downcast, and unsmiling woman.

Less than a week after Pierre's funeral, Marie retreated to her laboratory. She had wondered whether she would be able to continue the work she and Pierre had begun, but discovered that she felt closest to him at her work desk. When the French government offered her a widow's pension, she refused it, saying, "I am young enough to earn my living and that of my children."

Pierre's brother Jacques and Bronya felt the University of Paris had an obligation to help Marie. They visited the Dean of the Science School and asked that she be allowed to continue with the research work she and Pierre had begun, as well as be asked to teach her late husband's physics course. The Dean concurred. Marie would be the first woman professor and chief of research at La Sorbonne. The position paid an annual salary of 10,000 francs.

Marie hesitated before accepting the offer, but she remembered Pierre's words: "Whatever happens, even if one has to go on like a body without a soul, one must work just the same...." Marie wrote in her journal that she accepted the offer, and to her father-in-law, she said, "I will try."

Slowly, Marie stepped back into her old routine. She spent hours in the laboratory and stayed in Paris most of the summer, preparing notes for the physics class she would teach in the fall. When her schedule allowed, she rode out to the countryside to spend time with her daughters, who were staying with Marie's sister, Hela, and Dr. Curie.

In the fall, Marie decided to move to her husband's native community of Sceaux. Her commute to the University would be longer, but living in a small town meant more space and security for her children.

On November 5, 1906, almost six months after her husband's death, Marie stood for the first time at the podium in the physics lecture hall filled with students, photographers, colleagues, and spectators eager to hear and see the first woman teach at the famed Sorbonne. Marie entered the auditorium quietly and without ceremony and addressed the class in a clear and precise voice. She began teaching the lesson at the precise point where Pierre had left off six months earlier. At the conclusion of her lecture she left the podium to the thunder of applause.

In 1910, Marie applied for membership in the prestigious Academy of Sciences, the leading scientific society in France. While many of her colleagues rallied around her, others opposed allowing a woman entry into France's preeminent scientific organization. In the end, the old guard won and Marie was refused admission.

In that same year Dr. Eugene Curie died at age eighty-two. He had been a devoted grandfather to Irene and Eve. As always, Marie's work sustained her through a difficult time. She was also involved in discussions about the possibility of forming an institute to honor Pierre's work and memory. The Pasteur Institute and the University of Paris

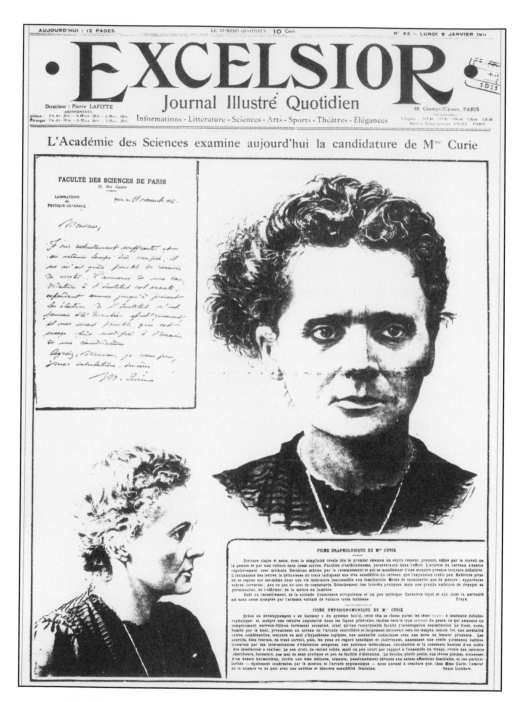

Horrified that a woman would presume to request admittance to the lauded Academy of Sciences, Excelsior printed this article claiming to analyze Marie's facial features and handwriting. The "analysis" claimed that Marie Sklodowska Curie was probably Jewish and unworthy of the honor. (Duke University)

were interested in jointly funding a place for the study of radioactivity, as well as a medical research facility. The two buildings would sit next to each other on university property, and together would be known as the Institut du Radium.

Marie was working on a book called *Treatise on Radioactivity* in which she recorded all the information that was known about radioactivity at that time. The nearly one-thousand-page book was published in 1910 and was well received by the scientific community.

Marie's long hours in the laboratory and classroom, combined with the toll taken by her grief, affected the time and attention she gave to her daughters. She struggled to balance her work and personal life, but her writings as well as those of her daughters reveal she did not always succeed. Her children often missed her. Although not an affectionate mother, she did work to provide a caring home, a good education, and a nourishing environment. Irene attended a private girls' school and, for a time, both Irene and Eve, along with the children of other scientists, were taught by a group of professors skilled in the fields of physics, chemistry, and mathematics. The girls also went on trips with friends and relatives and took excursions to the countryside.

Irene and Eve grew to realize how their father's death had altered Marie. She experienced a series of depressions and often collapsed from nervous exhaustion. She had no female colleagues, other than her sister Bronya, as confidants. Her days consisted of working with men who

Marie Curie (leaning on her elbow, to the right) at the Solvay conference. The two men at the far right are Albert Einstein, who became Curie's friend, and Paul Langevin. (Courtesy of the Association Curie et Joliot-Curie, Paris.)

sometimes resented her stubborn and determined nature. Most of the photographs taking during this period show Marie surrounded by men. In 1910, at the First Solvay conference on physics in Brussels, for example, a photograph shows Marie seated at a table with nearly twenty-five men around her. One of the men is a young physicist named Albert Einstein, the father of the theory of relativity, who would become her friend.

One of the most important issues discussed at the 1910 Solvay Conference was the need to establish an international radium standard. A standard would help insure that medical treatments were reliable and that radium was produced in consistent strengths. Marie said it was essential in order to "assure agreement between numerical results obtained in different laboratories." Laboratories around the world could compare their own preparations of radium and all experiments would be based on the same unit.

The International Radium Standards Committee agreed that the unit for radioactivity should be called a Curie in honor of Pierre Curie, but the amount of radioactivity to correspond with one Curie was undecided. At the time, a working amount of radium was only a few milligrams. Marie wanted a Curie to comprise a larger quantity. She was chosen to develop the standard.

Marie used a method called "emanation," which measures a quantity of radium by the amount of radioactive gas it produces. She told the International Radium Standards Committee in 1911 that the standard measurement of radium was a thin glass tube of twenty-one milligrams of pure radium salts. She asked to keep the tube in her laboratory "partly for sentimental reasons and partly to continue observations on its activity." The committee, however, decided the international standard should be registered with the Bureau of Weights and Measures at Sevres, and instructed Marie to deliver the glass vial there.

eight
PRIVATE LIFE, PUBLIC SCANDAL

    Although Marie worked long hours, she occasionally found time to socialize with friends and colleagues. One friend was physicist Paul Langevin, who had known both Marie and Pierre for a long time. Langevin, who would later help to design a sonar detector that was used to find German submarines during World War I, was married and had several children, but lived apart from his wife. Marie enjoyed talking to Langevin about science, something she had missed since Pierre's death. Eventually, their relationship became intimate. Their affair would soon damage her professional standing.

    In 1911, Marie was nominated by the Nobel Prize Committee for a second award, this time in Chemistry, for her work in isolating and purifying radium. The nomination was announced at the same time her relationship with

Paul Langevin, Curie family friend and mentor to Irene's future husband. (Bibliothèque nationale de France, Paris)

Langevin came to public attention. Those who viewed her romance with a married man as improper opposed her being granted a second Nobel Prize. This period in Marie's life tested her reserves of strength, courage, and dignity, but Marie had learned early on in life "to never . . . be beaten down by persons or events."

In the spring of 1911, personal letters Marie had written to Paul Langevin were stolen from his Paris apartment. Madame Langevin, Paul's estranged wife, had arranged

for someone to steal the letters. She was in the process of divorcing her husband and wanted proof of his infidelity.

Madame Langevin did not immediately reveal the contents of the letters to the newspapers. But in November 1911, while Marie was at the Solvay conference in Brussels, a Paris newspaper, *Le Journal*, ran an attention-grabbing headline: "A Story of Love: Madame Curie and Professor Langevin." The next day, a second paper picked up the story.

Marie ran into a public firestorm when she returned from the conference. She was besieged by reporters and critics. Even in the small town of Sceaux, outraged citizens walked by her house and shouted insults. Marie and her daughters fled their home to stay with friends in Paris. During the early 1900s in France, it was widely acknowledged that married men might have affairs. The same was not true for women, however, and Marie bore the brunt of the scandal.

As the newspapers were publicizing the affair, the Nobel Committee announced that Marie had won the prize. This second award recognized her discovery of radioactive elements as well as her success in obtaining a pure sample of radium and in determining its atomic weight. It was a great personal triumph, but Marie's joy was overshadowed by the scandal. The committee even sent an informal letter asking her not to attend the award ceremony.

Marie wrote back:

In fact the prize has been awarded for the discovery

of radium and polonium. I believe that there is no connection between my scientific work and the facts of private life…I cannot accept the idea in principle that the appreciation of the value of scientific work should be influenced by libel and slander concerning private life. I am convinced that this opinion is shared by many people. I am very saddened that you are not yourself of this opinion.

Although exhausted by the steady stream of criticism, Marie summoned inner reserves of strength and sent a telegram to the committee announcing that she would personally accept the award.

When she won one-fourth of the Nobel Prize for Physics in 1903, Curie became the first woman ever to receive the honor. In 1911, she was the sole winner of the Nobel Prize in Chemistry. Marie Curie became the first person to win or share two Nobel Prizes. She shares the distinction of getting two Nobel Prizes in two different categories with just one other person, Linus Pauling, who won for Chemistry and Peace. (© The Nobel Foundation 1911)

In December 1911, Marie traveled to Sweden with her two daughters and Bronya. The president of the Royal Swedish Academy of Sciences told the audience that the Award in Chemistry was for Marie Curie's valuable contribution to the understanding of atoms and radioactive elements. He also cited her previous work in the study of radium and polonium. In her acceptance speech, Marie thanked the Academy and said, "The award of this high distinction is motivated by common work and thus pays homage to the memory of Pierre Curie."

After the ceremony, Marie returned to France and moved to a large fourth floor apartment at 36 Quai de Bethune in Paris. She had decided to move from the house in Sceaux to better protect her family from reporters and photographers. Marie and Langevin remained friends and professional colleagues, but eventually ended their romance and Langevin returned to his wife.

In the months that followed, Marie fell into depression. Her weight dropped from 123 pounds to 103. Nevertheless, she continued to spend most days in her laboratory. Eventually, the pace of work caught up with her and her health failed. She suffered from high fevers and kidney problems severe enough to require surgery. When she was released from the hospital, she went to a private medical facility to recuperate.

Marie's daughters remained in Paris with a governess, but desperately wanted to see their mother. Marie would not allow them to visit because she did not want them to be upset by her condition, or to be taken away from their school and daily routine. They wrote her letters and she wrote back. Slowly, her health improved, and in August 1912, she went to England to stay with Hertha Ayrton, a friend and fellow scientist. Her girls were allowed to come to England and stay. Ayrton provided Marie and the children with excellent care and protection from the outside world.

By the fall of 1913, Marie had begun to regain her strength. She was only forty-six years old, but her frail, thin body and gray hair made her look older. She was able to travel to Warsaw, Poland to dedicate a radium institute, where she was made an honorary director. Her visit brought back many memories. Poland was still a poor and beaten-down country, but Marie hoped that one day her homeland would regain its freedom.

When Marie returned to Paris, she resumed her teaching and laboratory work. In addition, she began to plan the building of the Radium Institute, which was to be located in the rue Pierre Curie. It would have two laboratories, one for the study of radioactivity and the other for bio-logical and medical research. Marie was named director of the radioactivity laboratory; a physician named Claude Regaud was in charge of the medical laboratory. Both units would work for the development and advancement of radium science.

While the foundations for the institute were being laid, Marie worked on a small courtyard garden between the Curie and Pasteur pavilions. She planted willow and lime trees, shrubs, and a rose garden. As construction progressed,

The Radium Institute was founded with two concentrations: research and treatment. It now sees 75,000 patients every year. Marie's personal laboratory and office have been decontaminated (even her notebooks were radioactive) and preserved for the public. (Courtesy of the Association Curie et Joliot-Curie, Paris.)

she took an active part in meeting with the contractors and workers. She wanted the Institute and Curie Laboratory to reflect the high research standards she and Pierre had maintained in their shabby and poorly equipped laboratories. In his lifetime, Pierre had never had a suitable laboratory; Marie was determined that now that he was gone, a laboratory worthy of his work would be erected.

The Radium Institute was completed in July 1914. It had cost 800,000 francs to build. Marie planned to move her laboratory equipment from her old work space into the new, well-equipped Institute. But before she could move, the world began to collapse around her.

World War I began on August 4, 1914. Soon, German troops threatened Paris. Parisians fled by the thousands, but Marie refused to leave. She stayed at the Radium Institute to guard its most precious possession, a single gram of radium. She knew that even this tiny amount could be a lethal weapon in the wrong hands.

Marie decided to take the radium to Bordeaux for safekeeping. She traveled by train, carrying a heavy case with the vial of radium inside, protected by thick lead covers. When she arrived, Bordeaux was crowded with fleeing Parisians. Even the government of Paris had temporarily moved to Bordeaux. She delivered the package to a Bordeaux bank, where it was placed in a safety vault, and returned by train to Paris.

Marie's daughters, on summer vacation in Brittany with a governess, begged to rejoin their mother in Paris, but Marie would not allow it. She stayed in touch by writing letters that revealed her tender feelings for Irene and Eve. On August 31, 1914, she answered Irene's letter sent from Brittany.

> I have just received your sweet letter of Saturday, and I wanted so much to kiss you that I almost cried. Things are not going very well, and we are all heavyhearted and disturbed in soul. We need great courage, and I hope that we shall not lack it. We must keep our certainty that after the bad days the good times will come again. It is in this hope that I press you to my heart, my beloved daughters.

By October 1914, the French and British forces had secured Paris, and the girls returned home. Irene, now seventeen, was ready to enter college. Following in her mother's footsteps, she registered at La Sorbonne to study mathematics, physics, and chemistry and also took a course in nursing. Irene was a bright, private girl who showed great potential in science. Marie hoped that one day she might take over the directorship of the Curie Laboratory. Eve, who was nine, attended secondary school. A pretty, cheerful girl, she was more interested in music and literature than the sciences.

Marie had her daughters back with her, but life was far from normal. A terrible war had just begun and she wanted to find a way to serve her adopted country. She visited hospitals and asked about their X-ray equipment. She knew that this new technology could help doctors locate bullets and broken bones in wounded soldiers.

In 1896, a year after Wilhelm Röntgen had discovered X-rays, a machine to harness them was developed. X-ray machines work by directing a beam of high-speed electrons at an object. As the X-rays pass through the object, an image is captured on a photographic plate. By 1910, physicians who could afford them were purchasing X-ray machines. Marie found that many of the hospitals she visited did not have the machines. Even army field hospitals did not have the equipment, which meant surgeons on the front line could not use the technology to treat wounded soldiers.

Marie saw a way to help France's war effort. Other scientists were helping to develop new weapons, such as mustard gas. Marie refused to use her knowledge for destructive purposes, a principle she adhered to throughout her life. She once said, "Our special duty is to aid those to whom we think we can be most useful."

There was no one to staff the new laboratory at the Radium Institute. Everyone was fighting the war. There was still a great deal of work to do, but she set this task aside and turned her energies to the war effort.

Marie began working to get X-ray machines and other equipment to the military field hospitals. She went to the French government and asked for an official title: Director of the Red Cross Radiology Service. Next, she appealed to The Union of Women of France to finance the purchase of a motor-touring car. The women raised the funds and Marie painted a red cross on the car and outfitted it with a small generator, a movable tray, a folding table, photographic plates, an X-ray tube, and all the items needed to make X-ray images of wounds. By the end of October 1914, Marie had assembled the first vehicle with full X-ray capability. She also learned how to drive, and even studied auto mechanics in case the car broke down. She taught herself how to operate the X-ray equipment and then trained volunteers to use it.

The X-ray car was dubbed a Petite Curie. Marie knew she needed many more of them. She appealed to anyone who had a car to donate it and asked for contributions of money, laboratory, and other scientific equipment. Eventually, she outfitted twenty Petite Curies that were used to set up X-ray facilities along the front lines. Now soldiers who

Marie drove the Petite Curie to hospitals, and used the mobile X-ray unit to diagnose many wounded soldiers. (Courtesy of the Association Curie et Joliot-Curie, Paris.)

fell in battle could be examined and their wounds properly diagnosed. Marie's efforts saved the lives and limbs of thousands of soldiers wounded during World War I.

Marie made several trips to field hospitals in France and Belgium. She traveled over bumpy and muddy roads, hunched over the steering wheel. Upon arrival at her destination, she unloaded the car, set up the table, and hooked up a cable to a generator she had brought with her. Then she would spend long hours taking X-rays of the wounded soldiers. Often, she stayed until she could train a person to do the work after she had gone.

In her *Autobiographical Notes*, Marie mentions how difficult it was to find assistants. Radiology was a new field and few people had the necessary medical knowledge. Marie appealed to the national Health Services department to make the study of radiology part of course work for nurses, which it did in 1916.

Marie was always exhausted. She did not have enough drivers or trained technicians to deliver and set up the equipment. Eventually, she turned to the one person she could trust to be careful and thorough—her daughter, Irene. They traveled to the battlefield hospitals where Marie showed Irene how to use the X-ray equipment. A strong bond of affection and respect developed between them during this time. They saw many terrible wounds, learned how to deal with difficult doctors skeptical of the use of X-rays, and coped with the almost overwhelming suffering around them. At age seventeen, Irene was even put in charge of a field radiology facility in Belgium while fighting raged close by. On her own, she X-rayed the wounded and then showed the surgeons where to make their incisions.

Irene spent her eighteenth birthday training nurses so that she could move on to the next battlefield station. She moved up the battle line, training more nurses and teaching herself how to repair X-ray equipment. In 1916, she returned to Paris and used her newly acquired knowledge to set up an X-ray training course for nurses at the Radium Institute. About one hundred fifty women graduated from the course and headed to the front lines. While Irene taught, she attended classes herself, and in 1917 she graduated from La

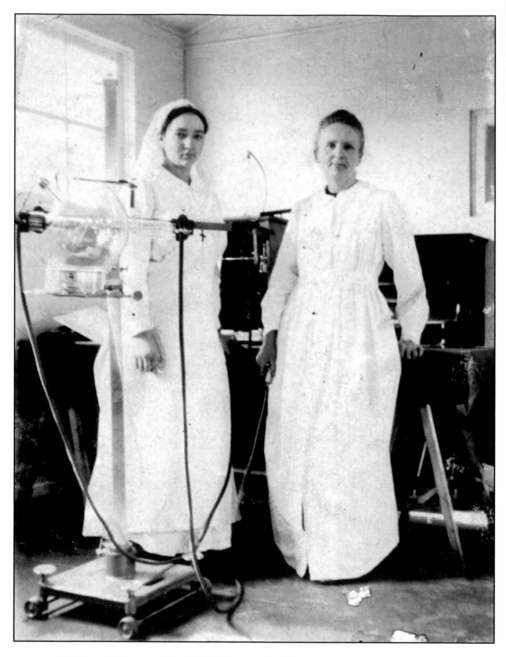

Marie and Irene at a hospital in Hoogstade, Belgium in 1915. (Courtesy of the Association Curie et Joliot-Curie, Paris.)

Sorbonne with honors in mathematics, chemistry and physics. She then became her mother's laboratory assistant.

Meanwhile, Marie was working with radium again. When the danger of a German invasion eased, she retrieved the gram of radium from Bordeaux. She was anxious to perform tests on radon, a radioactive gas, to see if it was easier to use than radium in the treatment of wounds. But first she needed to draw the gas off the radium, a task she accomplished with an electric pump that sealed the gas in thin glass tubes that could be placed inside a patient's body to get the radon closer to the wound site.

On November 11, 1918, Germany surrendered. World War I was finally over. The war had sapped Marie's energy and health, as well as the money she had invested in war bonds. She wanted to get back to her work at the Curie Laboratory, but first she needed a rest.

In the summer of 1919, Marie traveled to the village of Larcouest in Brittany, on the coast of the English Channel. It was one of her favorite vacation spots. She rented a house and spent time with her daughters, swimming, walking hillside trails, and visiting with friends who also vacationed at Larcouest.

At the end of the vacation, Marie returned to her work and to her plans for the Radium Institute and Curie Laboratory. Although the French government had contributed financial support, it was not enough money to build the Institute into a world-class research facility. Marie could raise money by giving speeches, but she was a private person who preferred the quiet and solitude of her laboratory. But there had to be funds for equipment, qualified scientists and assistants, and more radium. The war had almost bankrupted the French government. She would have to find a way to raise the money herself, but had no idea of how to do it. She was now fifty-one years old, and she wrote in her *Autobiographical Notes*:

> I am no longer young, and I frequently ask myself whether, in spite of recent efforts of the government aided by some private donations, I shall ever succeed in building up for those who will come after me an Institute of Radium, such as I wish to the memory of Pierre Curie and to the highest interest of humanity.

nine
AMERICA

Marie Curie was searching for help raising money to complete the institute when she met Marie Mattingly Meloney. Meloney, who was called Missy, was an American editor of a magazine called *Everybody's*. Soon after meeting Curie, she became editor of the *Delineator*, a leading women's magazine. Missy was married to another editor, William Brown Meloney. Her father had been a doctor who conducted research work and her mother was a writer who opened a school for freed slaves. Missy grew up in a home where education and individuality were encouraged. At the age of seventeen, she became a journalist at the *Washington Post*. She was in her twenties when Marie Curie discovered radium, and Missy had followed Marie's career with admiration.

When Missy was in her late thirties she wrote to Marie

Marie Curie, in a colorized photograph, looking much as she must have appeared to Missy Meloney. (Courtesy of the Granger Collection.)

requesting an interview, but Marie refused. Missy was persistent, however, and in May 1920, when she was traveling in Europe, she sent a letter through another scientist that read in part: "My father, who was a medical man, used to say that it was impossible to exaggerate the importance of people. But you have been important to me for twenty years, and I want to see you a few minutes."

Marie agreed to meet the American reporter in her office. She was then fifty-two years old, Missy was thirty-nine, but was gray-haired, and walked with a limp. Both women were determined and willing to work hard to achieve their goals. When Missy learned that Marie's laboratory had only one gram of radium, while American scientists had fifty times that amount, she was shocked. How could the woman who had discovered radium have less in her laboratory than other scientists? The answer was simple—Marie Curie did not have enough money to buy radium, which sold for around $100,000 a gram.

"You ought to have all the resources in the world to continue your research. Someone must undertake this," Missy declared. She offered to raise money in the United States to buy radium for Marie's laboratory. She was confident American women would support such an effort.

Missy outlined a plan. She would handle the fundraising efforts by promising donors that Marie would come speak or visit their organization. Once the money was raised, Marie would travel to the United States to receive the radium, make some speeches, visit a few colleges, and attend dinners in her honor. It would be an opportunity to tour the country. Marie considered Missy's offer. She needed more radium to continue her research, and it could be a pleasant diversion to visit Niagara Falls and the Grand Canyon. On the other hand, her health was poor and

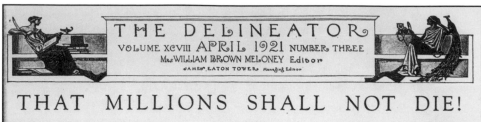

THE DELINEATOR

VOLUME XCVIII APRIL 1921 NUMBER THREE

Mrs. WILLIAM BROWN MELONEY Editor

JAMES EATON TOWER Managing Editor

THAT MILLIONS SHALL NOT DIE!

EVERY little while a man or a woman is born to serve in some big way, and such a one is Marie Curie, the discoverer of radium, whose story THE DELINEATOR publishes this month.

Madame Curie is not only great because of her contribution to science, but because of the spirit in which she bestowed her gift upon the world.

When the editor of THE DELINEATOR sought Madame Curie in Paris it was only with the idea of preparing an article for the two million women who read THE DELINEATOR.

A woman's magazine should be an institution of service, and the editor of THE DELINEATOR saw an opportunity for real service, not merely to the great Curie, but to mankind and particularly to womankind, many of whose physical ills may be solved by this woman's work.

But Madame Curie has no radium with which to experiment.

The money turned over to her for her work by foreign governments, the French Government, the Carnegie Foundation and the Nobel Prize Foundation, has been used by her in her investigations.

France is poor and there is less than a gram of radium at the Radium Institute in Paris, and this is needed for hospital use. While the French Government recently ordered two additional grams of radium, these too are for hospital use only and will not make it possible for Madame Curie to further her service to humanity by a possibly successful experiment. The opportunity for service which the editor of THE DELINEATOR saw, lay in providing Madame Curie with the radium she needs to continue her experiments.

One appeal to the readers of THE DELINEATOR would probably have raised the full amount. It was not necessary to make an appeal in the press.

The editor of THE DELINEATOR brought the facts to the attention of a group of representative American women, who pledged themselves to collect the required sum—one hundred and thirty thousand dollars.

It has been one of the dreams of Madame Curie to some day visit the United States. She is particularly interested in the radium activities here, the laboratories where original research work is being done, the pitchblende fields of Colorado, where Mother Earth has hidden the greatest known wealth of unrefined radium. But the country itself interests her. She has for many years wanted to see the Grand Cañon of the Colorado.

The great Curie has been asked to come to America to receive from American women the gift of a gram of radium which shall be hers, unrestricted, for experimental work.

CONTENTS

Among the scientists in America who are supporting this undertaking and who will receive Madame Curie when she arrives in this country are:

Dr. F. C. Wood of the Crocker Memorial Cancer-Research Laboratory; Dr. Will J. Mayo, President of the American Medical Association; Dr. Duane of Harvard; Dr. Robert Abbe of New York, who was the first surgeon in this country to work with radium; Dr. William Taylor of Philadelphia, president of the Medical College of the University of Pennsylvania; Dr. James Ewing of Cornell University; Professor Pegram of Columbia University; Dr. Carrel and Dr. Simon Flexner of the Rockefeller Institute; Dr. Greenough of Harvard; Dr. Taussig and Dr. Franklin H. Martin.

The small group of women who have formed the organization to assure the gift of radium to Madame Curie for experimental work are:

Madame Jusserand, Mrs. Robert Mead, Mrs. Edward H. Harkness, Mrs. V. Everit Macy, Mrs. John D. Rockefeller, Jr., Miss Florence Marshall, Mrs. Arthur Woods, Miss Mina Bruère, Mrs. William Vaughn Moody, Mrs. W. B. Meloney, Mrs. Robert Woods Bliss, and Mrs. Vernon Kellogg.

Mrs. Robert G. Mead, who is the secretary of the committee, founded the American Society for Control of Cancer. She has been identified with scientific and philanthropic work started in New York, which has developed into nation-wide significance.

With fine understanding, the group of American women who undertook to complete the purchase of radium for Madame Curie resolved that no one should be asked to add a dollar to the fund—only those who felt it a privilege to contribute would be permitted to add to the gift of American women to the world's great woman.

The Equitable Trust Company was appointed the depository of all money raised by the committee, and a trust was established in the name of the Marie Curie Radium Fund.

Madame Curie made no appeal for this help. She would never consent to a request for financial assistance being made in her name. In a recent letter to the editor of THE DELINEATOR she said:

"It is true that I am not rich, but that is nearly always the case with French scientists and I live like other professors of the University; so I do not complain or feel unhappy about it. My gift to the Radium Institute was not so much in money as in radium produced by me."

It is characteristic of this great woman to speak lightly of her priceless gift, but time must not slip by without opportunity being given her to do the only thing she asks to do—render further service to humanity.

OUR UNITED STATES BRANCHES:

2231-2249 South Park Avenue - - - - - Chicago, Ill.
605 Mission Street - - - - - San Francisco, Cal.
70-72 Marietta Street - - - - - - Atlanta, Ga.
18 Chauncy Street - - - - - - Boston, Mass.
1114-16 Washington Avenue - - - - - St. Louis, Mo.

Published monthly by THE BUTTERICK PUBLISHING CO.

George W. Wilder, President   William A. Publow, Secretary
Charles D. Wilder, Treasurer

Butterick Building, Spring and Macdougal Streets, New York

OUR FOREIGN OFFICES:

27 Avenue de l'Opéra - - - - - - - Paris, France
83 and 84 Long Acre - - - - London, W. C., England
468 Wellington Street, West - - - Toronto, Ontario, Canada
319 Elgin Avenue - - - - - Winnipeg, Manitoba, Canada

TERMS OF SUBSCRIPTION: The price of THE DELINEATOR is two dollars and fifty cents per year, or twenty-five cents per copy in the United States, Alaska, Cuba, Porto Rico, the Virgin Islands, Mexico, Hawaii, Philippines, Panama, Guam, Tutuila, and the city of Shanghai; in Canada, three dollars per year, or twenty-five cents per copy; in other countries, three dollars and fifty cents per year for subscription, or thirty cents per copy. All Rural Free Carriers can supply postal money-order for the renewal of subscriptions. Subscriptions are registered within three days after their receipt by us. We always date from the current issue, unless otherwise instructed. We can not acknowledge single subscriptions. We should be notified of any change of address between the fifteenth and the twenty-second of second preceding month of issue. When you order a change, be sure to give the old as well as new address. If your magazine fails to arrive, advise us by postal. To avoid confusion always sign your name the same as signed when forwarding the subscription. As an example, if your order is given in the name of Mrs. John Jones, do not write later in the name of Mrs. Mary P. Jones. The editors assume no risk for manuscripts and illustrations submitted to this magazine, but will use all due care while they are in their hands.

Missy Meloney's April 1921 Delineator *article.* (State Library of North Carolina)

her work was pressing. She finally agreed to stay in the United States for only a few weeks. Missy headed home to organize the first fund-raiser.

Missy Meloney's first step was to write an article for the *Delineator* magazine that painted a picture of Marie Curie as a hardworking scientist and mother who had won two Nobel Prizes for the discovery of radium, a powerful radioactive element that held the promise of curing cancer. Though Marie was a heroine and role model for women around the world, she did not have the resources to buy a mere gram of radium for her own laboratory. It was an effective beginning to the fund-raising campaign.

In the process of raising the funds, Missy sometimes presented a distorted picture of Marie Curie's life. Missy wrote colorful, compelling stories about Marie's struggles with widowhood and her difficulties mothering two girls when work and war separated them for long periods of time. While it was true Marie loved her daughters and disliked being away from them, she accepted the separations as unavoidable if she was to complete her work.

Missy worked to soften the hearts of Americans and to encourage them to open their purses. She portrayed Marie as a poor and needy scientist, although she earned a good salary as a university professor and director of the Curie Laboratory, lived in a nice apartment and paid for occasional vacations.

Exaggerating Marie's poverty was one thing, but Missy also claimed that Marie had found a potential cure for cancer. Marie had never said that cancer could be cured with radium and had told Missy that, although she was interested in the medical uses of radium, she was not directly involved in developing cancer treatments. Her interest was in researching the properties of radium and the structure of the atom. A separate branch of the Radium Institute, under the direction of Dr. Claude Regaud, offered early radium treatment, called "Curietherapy" in France.

The treatment of cancer with radiation offered promise, but little was known about its long-term effects on the human body. Although Marie had not protected herself against radiation overexposure, she knew that people had died as a result of radiation poisoning. Marie did not point to radium as the cause of her own health problems, but did write in her *Autobiographical Notes* that, "since the handling of radium is far from being free of danger (several times I have felt a discomfort which I consider a result of this cause)" she was taking measures to prevent harmful effects on laboratory assistants and nurses who handled radioactive materials.

Missy Meloney was a clever fund-raiser who enlisted the help of men and women from all walks of life. She appealed to doctors, scientists, lawyers, women's rights leaders, socialites, and civic activists to help raise money for the "Marie Curie Radium Fund." In less than a year, Missy and her committees raised the $100,000 to buy Marie's laboratory a gram of radium.

In early spring 1921, Marie sailed for America on the steamship *Olympic* with her daughters. Missy was on board with them. Marie was almost fifty-four years old, her daughter Irene almost twenty-four, and Eve sixteen. Marie's eyesight was poor and she had a loud, persistent ringing in her ears. The trip was an ordeal, but she had made a promise. In Paris she had tried to keep a schedule

The travelers aboard the Olympic. *From left to right: Missy Meloney, Irene, Marie, and Eve Curie.* (Library of Congress)

that would have been punishing even for a younger person in good health.

Marie, visibly nervous at sea, stayed in her cabin for most of the ocean voyage. Irene and Eve, on the other hand, were excited. They had bought new clothes and were looking forward to seeing New York and touring the United States. Eve, in particular, was a vivacious teenager who liked to meet people, dance, dress up, and have fun. She was more outgoing than either her mother or sister.

When the ship docked in New York, a crowd of newspaper reporters, journalists, and photographers rushed on board to interview the important scientist. They had read so much about her in the past year that they were eager to ask her questions and take photographs. An overwhelmed Marie sat huddled in a chair on the ship's deck, dressed in dark clothes with a small hat perched on her head, a purse clutched to her chest. The flash bulbs hurt her eyes, and her ears were filled with buzzing noises. She asked the photographers to leave and then politely answered the reporters' questions.

After the boisterous welcome, Marie's visit to the United States was a pleasant, if exhausting, trip. In her *Autobiographical Notes*, she wrote that, "during all that travel I was protected with the greatest care, in order to lighten as far as possible the inevitable fatigue of the voyage and the receptions. America not only gave me a generous welcome, but also true friends whom I could not thank enough for their kindness and their devotion."

Marie's public image had changed dramatically from a decade earlier, when her affair had become public. Now, newspapers around the world carried the story of America welcoming the famous scientist with open arms.

Marie was kept busy with speaking engagements at women's colleges in New York and New England, where girls surrounded her with warm greetings. She wrote that she was impressed with the "care of the health and the physical development of the students, and the very independent organization of their life which allows a large degree of individual initiative." There were also visits to research laboratories, science organizations and women's clubs, receptions at museums, and awards dinners where Marie, dressed in a collegiate cap and gown, accepted honorary degrees and medals. She shook so many hands that her fragile arm became sprained; she continued the trip with it in a sling. At times Irene or Eve stepped in so that their mother could rest and regain her strength. Along the way, Marie enjoyed a visit to Niagara Falls, and her daughters were entertained with tennis, boating, and swimming trips.

Finally, on May 20, Marie traveled to the White House to accept the gram of radium from President Harding. Marie described it in her notes as, "A remembrance never to be forgotten in which the chief representative of a great nation offered me homage of infinite value, the testimonial of the recognition of his country's citizens."

Actually, the radium was not brought to the ceremony because of safety concerns. Instead, the President presented Marie with a small golden key that opened the leaden case containing the radium. The tubes of radium had been left in a Pittsburgh processing factory for Marie to retrieve when she was ready to leave the country. The White House ceremony was followed with a reception at the French and Polish embassies.

Marie Curie, descending the steps of the White House with U.S. president Warren Harding. (Library of Congress)

Marie thanked everyone in her quiet way. Dressed in her customary black attire, she spoke a few words and then took her seat. Afterward, she was exhausted and eager to return to France, but first she and her daughters traveled to the western United States, where they toured the Rocky Mountains and the Grand Canyon. Marie was content to sightsee, but the young girls rode mules to the bottom of the canyon. Marie also managed to visit a factory where radium was extracted from ore using the process Marie had developed.

On June 28, 1921, Marie and her daughters returned to France on the same ship that had taken them to New York. Marie had been away for nearly two months. One benefit of the trip was the establishment of a New York-based Marie Curie Radium Fund that would earn interest and provide her with a regular income. She ended her *Autobiographical Notes* by writing:

> I got back to France with a feeling of gratitude for the precious gift of the American women, and with a feeling of affection for their great country tied with ours by a mutual sympathy which gives confidence in a peaceful future for humanity.

She would make one more trip to America, in 1929. She went to raise money to purchase more radium, this time for the Radium Institute of Warsaw, Poland, and also to be entertained at the White House by President Hoover.

ten

RADIUM INSTITUTE

Marie's biggest concern during the last ten years of her life was the Radium Institute. For many years she had suffered health problems, including hand blisters and burns, aching bones and muscles, and kidney and liver problems. She hinted that radium was the culprit when she wrote to her sister Bronya that, "Perhaps radium has something to do with these troubles, but it cannot be affirmed with certainty."

As Marie aged, her health worsened. She developed cataracts in both eyes and underwent four surgeries to remove them. Frequently depressed and constantly tired, she nevertheless continued her work as director of the Curie Laboratory. There were days when she could hardly tear herself away from analyzing and measuring radioactive elements and their properties. When she was not working or helping researchers and students, she prepared lessons and lectured at La Sorbonne.

Although Marie devoted most of her time to researching radioactive elements, she was intrigued with the work being done on the structure of atoms. Years before she had hypothesized that there was some unknown phenomenon going on in the interior of the atom that caused radioactivity. It was later confirmed that radioactivity was actually tiny particles emanating from the atom's nucleus. It would have been logical for Marie to expand her research into this area, and many of her colleagues and assistants thought she should spend more time researching atomic structure. But Marie did not have the energy to pursue the new field of nuclear energy. However, she offered her help and advice whenever asked.

Marie groomed Irene to assume her research and to direct the Radium Institute. Irene worked as Marie's laboratory assistant and had done doctoral research work on the alpha rays of polonium. She was a careful scientist who worked long hours, but was not popular with the other laboratory workers. She was not warm and outgoing, and rarely spoke to colleagues. There was grumbling among the staff that her mother favored her too much. Actually, Irene was similar to her mother. Both were reserved, tough, and determined women who had high standards for themselves as well as for others. Marie did not hesitate to fire someone if their work fell short of her expectations, and Irene was all business as soon as she walked into the laboratory.

In 1924, Marie hired a young physicist named Frederic

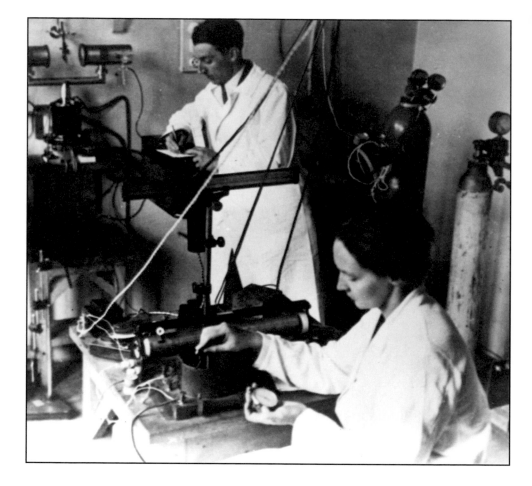

Irene Curie and Frederic Joliot at work in the laboratory. (Courtesy of the Association Curie et Joliot-Curie, Paris.)

Joliot. He was an intelligent, charming man who had studied under Paul Langevin at the School of Industrial Physics and Chemistry of the City of Paris (EPCI). Marie gave Irene the job of teaching Joliot the laboratory routines and procedures for working with radium. As Marie watched the young couple develop a working relationship, it must have reminded her of her own partnership with Pierre. Yet when Irene and Joliot announced their intention to marry, Marie warned Irene that Joliot might be more interested in attaching himself to the Curie family name than to Irene herself. True to her steadfast nature, Irene held her ground and married Joliet on October 9, 1926, in a civil ceremony. Eve served them a wedding lunch, and then the newlyweds returned to their work in the laboratory. Over the next few years, Marie insisted that her son-in-law pursue his education. He earned a second baccalaureate, followed by a bachelor's degree and doctorate and became an excellent physicist and chemist. Moreover, he and Irene dined with her mother three nights a week.

In 1927 Irene gave birth to a baby girl whom she named Helene. She was Marie's first grandchild. Shortly after the baby was born, Irene went back to work and a nursemaid took care of the infant. When Irene's second child, Pierre, was born five years later, she worked until a few hours before his birth.

In 1932, Marie decided to hand over the directorship of the Curie Laboratory to Irene. Marie encouraged her daughter and son-in-law to continue the research on radioactive materials and gave them polonium to work with. Eventually, they prepared and isolated a large and powerful amount of pure polonium. Irene and Frederic were also interested in duplicating the experiment of two German scientists who were studying the reactions of a radioactive substance when its particles hit a non-radioactive one.

Marie, Irene, Helene, Pierre, Frederic, and his mother enjoy an outing in the garden. Helene, a gifted scientist in her own right, eventually married Michel Langevin, Paul Langevin's grandson. (Courtesy of the Association Curie et Joliot-Curie, Paris.)

After conducting their own experiments, the Joliot-Curies, as they now called themselves, thought they had found something new about the source of radiation. They wrote a paper called "The Emission of Protons of Great Speed...Under the Influence of Gamma Rays."

Ernest Rutherford, the famous scientist who had discovered the nuclear structure of atoms, was skeptical about their findings. He did not believe that gamma rays played a part in radioactivity and asked his assistant, James Chadwick, to look into the research conducted by the Germans and

ERNEST RUTHERFORD AND THE NUCLEUS

Ernest Rutherford made many of the most critical discoveries in the early years of nuclear physics. He began his productive career studying with J. J. Thomson at Cambridge University and later moved into prestigious teaching and research positions and helped to train the next generation of researchers.

In 1898 Rutherford discovered that there was both positive and negative radiation, which he called alpha rays and beta rays. He later learned that radioactive elements deteriorate over time until they become lead. This deterioration happens at a regular rate, or half-life, which can be measured. This began the technique of radioactive dating that gives a much more accurate approximation of the age of the earth.

Rutherford is most famous for developing the nuclear model of the atom. Previous to the experiments Rutherford and his assistants carried out at Manchester University in Great Britain, most researchers accepted the "plum pudding" model of the atom put forth by J. J. Thomson. In this model it was thought that the positive and negative particles in an atom were spread fairly consistently throughout, like raisins in a plum pudding.

But after Rutherford and his team conducted experiments in which alpha particles were fired at a thin strip of gold film, it was discovered that all alpha particles did not perform the same way. Some penetrated the film, some bounced off like a rubber ball hitting a wall, and others scattered at wide angles. If the atom was structured as consistently as the plum pudding model said, the reaction of the alpha particles should have more uniformity. Rutherford concluded that most of the mass and charge of an electron is centered in one location, a nucleus, and particles orbit the nucleus like planets orbiting the sun. Instead of a plum pudding, most of the atom is empty space with a core consisting of a nucleus of tightly bound particles, orbited by electrons.

the Joliot-Curies. In the process, Chadwick discovered the neutron, a subatomic particle inside the nucleus of the atom. He later won a Nobel Prize for this discovery. The Joliot-Curies had been close to discovering the neutron, but had not completely understood the results of their experiments. Although they were disappointed, they continued with their work and soon made an important discovery.

In 1932 a new atomic particle was discovered by an American researcher, Carol Anderson. He called the positively charged particles "positrons." The Joliot-Curies immediately began bombarding a number of elements with alpha particles from polonium in search of positrons. One of the materials they used was aluminum foil. After the foil was bombarded, a Geiger counter measurement discovered that, even after the polonium was withdrawn, the aluminum still registered intense radioactivity for a full three minutes. The once-stable aluminum had become artificially radioactive.

The Joliot-Curies repeated their experiment several times and got the same result. They asked Marie to come and observe their experiment. Marie concurred that the Joilot-Curies had discovered a new type of artificial radioactivity.

This discovery was an important step in the development of nuclear physics. Now, instead of using the long and expensive process of separating and isolating natural radioactive elements from uranium or other ores, artificial radioactive isotopes could be produced in the laboratory.

These artificial radioactive isotopes would eventually lead to advances in medicine, research, and warfare.

Irene and Frederic had made a significant discovery, just as Marie and Pierre had done in the early 1900s. Frederic Joliot said, "I will never forget the expression of intense joy which came over her [Marie] when Irene and I showed her the first artificially radioactive element in a little glass tube."

In 1934 Marie was sixty-six years old. She still went to her laboratory, or visited the small garden she had planted between the Radium and Pasteur Institutes. She had moved to a new Paris apartment on the Quai de Bethune and was planning to build a modest country house in Sceaux.

Marie left her laboratory one day in May with a high fever and chills. She walked into the small courtyard garden to look at the rose bushes. When she arrived at home she went to bed and could not get up again. Doctors were called in and Marie was diagnosed with bronchitis, but they were not sure what was causing the high fever. They suggested she go to a sanitarium in the French Alps. Eve accompanied her very ill mother on the trip, and Irene followed at a later date.

Marie stayed in the sanitarium for two months, but her condition did not improve. Her fever remained high because she was suffering from a blood disorder called aplastic pernicious anemia. Her bone marrow had been damaged by years of unprotected exposure to radiation and could no longer produce healthy red blood cells. She fell into a coma and, on July 4, 1934, Marie Curie died. Irene, Eve, and Frederic were at her bedside. Later, she was buried next to Pierre in the cemetery at Sceaux.

Unfortunately, radium and X-ray exposure also caused Irene to later suffer severe health problems. At first Irene ignored her illnesses but eventually had to retreat to sanitariums to regain her strength. Doctors warned her to reduce her workload, but Irene felt she had the huge responsibility of following in her mother's footsteps as director of the Curie Laboratory.

In 1935, Irene and Frederic were nominated for the Nobel Prize in Chemistry for their discovery of artificial radiation. Irene gave an acceptance speech along with her husband. In 1936 the French government appointed her Undersecretary of State for Scientific Research and later asked her to serve on the Commission for Atomic Energy. In 1937 she was named Professor in the Faculty of Science at La Sorbonne.

Although she was a talented scientist and teacher, she was, like her mother, denied entrance in the French Academy of Sciences. It would take another forty years for the Academy to begin admitting women.

On March 17, 1956, Irene Joliot-Curie died at the age of fifty-nine from leukemia. Her husband Frederic died two years later from liver disease caused by unprotected exposure to radioactive materials. It was, he wryly noted, the family's "occupational disease."

Irene's daughter, Helene Langevin-Joliot, was the third generation of Curie women to work in the field of physics. She became a prominent scientist and teacher at the

Institute of Nuclear Physics at the University of Paris at Orsay.

Marie's younger daughter, Eve Curie, contributed to the family legacy by writing a biography of her mother called *Madame Curie*. It won the National Book Award and has been translated into thirty-two languages. It is a daughter's tribute to a woman scientist who made a career for herself in a profession dominated by men, a wife who lost her joy in life after the loss of her husband, and a mother who labored to raise two children on her own.

Today, the Radium Institute has been renamed the Curie Institute and is flourishing. It employs some four hundred people in its research division and another nine hundred in its medical division. Three thousand new cancer patients are treated there each year.

For more than forty years, radium was used to treat cancer and other illnesses. Today, other sources of radiation, such as cobalt isotopes, are available. The study of the atom and the knowledge that radioactivity comes from within the atom led to the development of the atomic bomb as well as nuclear energy. Marie and Pierre Curie realized early in their research that radioactive elements could be put to both positive and destructive uses. They were scientists but also humanitarians, pragmatic but hopeful, and they repeatedly cautioned that radium and other radioactive materials should be used to the benefit of mankind. As Pierre said in the acceptance speech for his Nobel Prize, "I am one of those who believe with Nobel

Alongside national heroes such as novelist Victor Hugo, Marie and Pierre were laid to rest in France's Pantheon. (Library of Congress)

that mankind will derive more good than harm from the new discoveries."

In the spring of 1995, President François Mitterrand of France placed the remains of Marie and Pierre Curie in a crypt in the country's treasured Pantheon, a place where the nation's great leaders are buried. Marie was the first woman awarded such recognition.

President Mitterrand said in his speech that the ceremony was "a deliberate outreach on our part from the Pantheon to the first lady of our honored history. It is another symbol that captures the attention of our nation and the exemplary struggle of a woman who decided to impose her abilities in a society where abilities, intellectual exploration, and public responsibility were reserved for men."

Marie's new resting place in the Pantheon, the Curie Institute, and all that she discovered and contributed will ensure that no one forgets this determined woman who wanted nothing more than to be a successful scientist, and prevailed beyond anything she might have imagined as a little girl called Manya.

Timeline

1867	Marie Curie is born in Warsaw, Poland, on November 7.
1877	Mother dies from tuberculosis.
1883	Graduates from high school with a gold medal for excellence.
1886	Begins a governess position with the Zorawski family.
1891	Arrives in Paris, France to attend La Sorbonne.
1893	Graduates first in her class and receives a degree in physics.
1894	Meets physicist Pierre Curie and earns a second degree in mathematics.
1895	Marries Pierre Curie on July 26.
1897	Daughter Irene is born on September 12. Marie also begins work for a doctorate degree.

1898	Discovers two new radioactive chemical elements and names them polonium and radium. Coins the term "radioactivity."
1901	Isolates a small amount of pure radium salts.
1903	Awarded the doctor of physical science degree and, along with Pierre Curie and Henri Becquerel, wins the Nobel Prize in Physics for their work on radioactivity.
1904	Daughter Eva is born on December 6.
1906	On April 19, Pierre Curie is killed in an accident on the streets of Paris. Marie becomes the first female professor at La Sorbonne.
1910	Publishes a one-thousand-page book called *Treatise on Radioactivity*.
1911	Prepares a standard measurement of radium and wins a second Nobel Prize in Chemistry for the refinement of pure radium.
1912	Falls seriously ill after years of working with radioactive materials.
1914	Begins work to build and develop a Radium Institute in Paris. When it is finished, Marie becomes director of the Curie Laboratories. World War I begins, and Marie helps the war effort by driving X-ray equipment to field hospitals.
1920	Meets an American reporter and fund-raiser named Missy Meloney.

1921	Travels to America to receive a gram of radium purchased with money raised by Meloney and other Americans.
1929	Makes a second trip to America to raise money for the Radium Institute of Warsaw, Poland.
1932	Hands over the directorship of the Curie Laboratory at the Radium Institute to her daughter Irene.
1934	Dies on July 4 and is buried in the Sceaux cemetery.
1995	Remains interred in the Pantheon.

Sources

CHAPTER ONE: A Girl Called Manya

p. 11, "Beg pardon! . . ." Eve Curie, *Madame Curie* (New York: Da Capo Press, second edition, 2001), 9.

p. 12, "That's stupid! . . ." Ibid., 27.

p. 21, "There are always a great . . ." Susan Quinn, *Marie Curie, A Life* (Massachusetts: Perseus Books, 1995), 54.

p. 22, "I have been to a kulig . . ." Ibid., 57.

CHAPTER TWO: Finding a Way

p. 25, "When you are a doctor . . ." Eve Curie, *Madame Curie*, 57.

p. 25, "What is your business, Mademoiselle? . . ." Ibid., 59.

p. 27, "One must not enter into contact . . ." Barbara Goldsmith, *Obsessive Genius: The Inner World of*

Marie Curie. (New York: W.W. Norton & Company, 2005), 36.

p. 30, "Don't believe the report of my approaching marriage . . ." Eve Curie, Madame Curie, 77.

p. 31, ". . . with my head high," Ibid., 41.

p. 31, "And now you, my little Manya: you must make something of . . ." Ibid., 83-84.

p. 32, "I have been stupid . . ." Ibid., 84.

p. 34, "If you can't see a way . . ." Goldsmith, Obsessive Genius, 43.

p. 35, "Now Bronya, I ask you for a definite answer . . ." Eve Curie, Madame Curie, 88.

p. 35, ". . . so nervous at the prospect . . ." Ibid., 89.

p. 35, "Nothing in life is to be feared . . ." Barbara Goldsmith, "I Found My Heroine" (New York: Parade Magazine, November 28, 2004), 4.

CHAPTER THREE: The Heroic Period

p. 39, "the heroic period . . ." Naomi Pasachoff, Marie Curie and the Science of Radioactivity (New York: Oxford University Press, 1996), 25.

p. 40, "working a thousand times as hard as at the beginning of my stay . . ." Quinn, A Life, 90.

p. 40-41, "Life is not easy for any of us . . ." Eve Curie, Madame Curie, 158.

p. 41, "All that I saw and learned . . ." Ibid., 85.

p. 42, "When one is young and solitary . . ." Ibid., 117.

p. 44, "Upon entering the room . . ." Marie Curie, *Pierre Curie with Autobiographical Notes by Marie Curie* (New York: Dover Publications, Inc., 1963), 85.

CHAPTER FOUR: Marie and Pierre

p. 46, "Women . . . draw us away from dedication . . ." Goldsmith, *Obsessive Genius*, 54.

p. 48, "To Mlle Sklodowska, with the respect . . ." Quinn, *A Life*, 116.

p. 48, "But you're coming back in October . . ." Eve Curie, *Madame Curie*, 129.

p. 48, "I hope you are laying up a stock of good air . . ." Ibid., 130.

p. 49, ". . .As you may imagine . . ." Ibid., 132.

p. 49, "Your letter worried me a great . . ." Ibid., 133

p. 50, "There isn't a soul on earth to equal . . ." Ibid., 134.

p. 50, "When you receive this letter . . ." Ibid., 136.

p. 54-55, "Everything goes well with us . . ." Ibid., 145-146.

p. 55, "My little girl, so dear, so sweet . . ." Ibid., 148.

CHAPTER FIVE: Radiation

p. 57, "I pray you to thank the Minister . . ." Marie Curie, *Autobiographical Notes*, 64.

p. 65, "I then made the hypothesis . . ." Goldsmith, *Obsessive Genius*, 77.

p. 67, "How glad I was when the sacks arrived . . ." Marie Curie, *Autobiographical Notes*, 91.

p. 69, "It was killing work to carry the receivers . . ." Eve Curie, *Madame Curie*, 170.

p. 71, "One of our joys was to go into our workroom at night . . ." Marie Curie, *Autobiographical Notes*, 92.

CHAPTER SIX: The Price of Fame

p. 77, "Our life has been altogether . . ." Eve Curie, *Madame Curie,* 217.

p. 79, "in the hands of criminals . . ." Quinn, *A Life*, 219.

p. 80, "We must make a living . . ." Goldsmith, *Obsessive Genius*, 125.

CHAPTER SEVEN: "I Will Try"

p. 85, "I do not understand that I am to live . . ." Eve Curie, *Madame Curie*, 254.

p. 86, "I am young enough to earn . . ." Ibid., 252.

p. 86, "Whatever happens, even if one . . ." Ibid., 254.

p. 86, "I will try . . ." Ibid., 253.

p. 91, "assure agreement between numerical . . ." Quinn, *A Life*, 345.

p. 91, "partly for sentimental reasons . . ." Ibid., 345.

CHAPTER EIGHT: Private Life, Public Scandal

p. 93, "to never . . . be beaten . . ." Goldsmith, "I Found My Heroine," 5.

p. 94, "A Story of Love . . ." Quinn, *A Life*, 302.

p. 94-95, "In fact the prize has been awarded . . ." Ibid., 328.

p. 96, "The award of this high distinction . . ." Pasachoff, *Science of Radioactivity*, 77.

p. 99, "I have just received your sweet letter . . ." Eve Curie, *Madame Curie*, 292.

p. 101, "Our special duty is to aid those . . ." Goldsmith, "I Found My Heroine," 5-6.

p. 106, "I am no longer young, and I frequently ask myself . . ." Marie Curie, *Autobiographical Notes*, 109-110.

CHAPTER NINE: America

p. 108-109, "My father, who was a medical man, used to say . . ." Eve Curie, *Madame Curie*, 322.

p. 109, "You ought to have all the resources . . ." Goldsmith, *Obsessive Genius*, 192.

p. 112, "Since the handling of radium . . ." Marie Curie, *Autobiographical Notes*, 107-108.

p. 114, "during all that travel I was protected . . ." Ibid., 113.

p. 115, "care of the health and the physical development . . ." Ibid., 113.

p. 155, "A remembrance never to be forgotten . . ." Ibid., 115.

p. 117, "I got back to France with a feeling of gratitude . . ." Ibid., 118.

CHAPTER TEN: Radium Institute

p. 118, "Perhaps radium has something to do . . ." Quinn, *A Life*, 416.

p. 125, "I will never forget the expression of intense joy . . ." Goldsmith, *Obsessive Genius*, 213.

p. 127-128, "I am one of those who believe . . ." Ibid., 128.

p. 128-129, ". . . a deliberate outreach on our part . . ." Ibid., 14-15.

Bibliography

Curie, Eve. *Madame Curie.* New York: Da Capo Press, 2001.

Curie, Marie. *Pierre Curie with Autobiographical Notes by Marie Curie.* New York: Dover Publications, Inc., 1963.

Flaum, Rosalynd P. *Marie Curie and Her Daughter Irene.* Minneapolis: Lerner Publications Company, 1993.

Goldsmith, Barbara. "I Found My Heroine." New York: Parade Magazine, November 28, 2004.

Goldsmith, Barbara. *Obsessive Genius: The Inner World of Marie Curie.* New York: W.W. Norton & Company, 2005.

Gribbin, John. *The Scientists.* New York: Random House, 2002.

Pasachoff, Naomi. *Marie Curie and the Science of Radio-activity.* New York: Oxford University Press, 1996.

Quinn, Susan. *Marie Curie, a Life.* Reading: Perseus Books, 1995.

Web sites

http://www.aip.org/history/curie/contents.htm
The American Institute of Physics maintains this site dedicated to the life of Marie Curie. Well-organized and packed with biographical information, including timelines, extensive articles, quotations, and photographs.

http://www.nobelprize.org/physics/articles/curie
The Nobel Prize Organization's official Web site features information about Marie and Pierre Curie's discovery of polonium and radium.

http://www.staff.amu.edu.pl/~zbzw/ph/sci/msc.htm
A detailed site offering a biographical overview of Marie Curie, as well as drawings of and facts about the elements radium and polonium.

http://www.physics.nist.gov/GenInt/Curie/1921.html
Marie Curie's visit to the United States is described in detail on site operated by the National Institute of Standards and Technology.

Index